12/88

St. Louis Community College
at Meramec
Library

FREEDOM FROM ANGER

THE DALDRUP METHOD

FREEDOM FROM
ANGER
THE DALDRUP METHOD

Dr. Roger J. Daldrup
and
Dodie Gust

Living Business Press
Aptos, California
1988

Copyright © 1988 by Roger J. Daldrup and Dodie Gust
All rights reserved.
Printed in the United States of America.
First Edition

Library of Congress
Catalog Card Number: 88-081097

Produced By: Catered Graphics
Executive Producers: Richard M. Ray and William M. Tomlinson
Cover Design: Russ Heinze and Roy Jones
Book Design: Janine M. Hunter
Production: Kathleen S. Parker
Typesetting: Linda Hernandez

This book is intended as a guide for personal growth and therapeutic work. Its proper application, as outlined in the book, should not be harmful to anyone.

The book is not, however, intended to take the place of professional counseling. And, as with other forms of therapy, applications of the book's suggestions could be abused, misused or otherwise employed in a way which could result in injury. Readers are urged to consult a qualified psychologist, psychiatrist or counselor to assist them in dealing with individual circumstances. The publisher, authors and their agents disclaim any and all liability or responsibility arising out of or in connection with the use of this book, its contents, the exercises contained in it, or the application of its principles to individual circumstances.

For my family, who paid the cost when I didn't free myself from my own anger.

— **Dr. Roger J. Daldrup**

For Lil Byers,
who has always loved me
unconditionally
— even through the angry years.

— **Dodie Gust**

CONTENTS

FOREWORD BY THE EDITOR

It was a sunny Sunday morning. My younger children, aged 6-point-9 and 8-and-a-half, as they'd tell me, sat with their Yahtzee game in front of the fireplace in the living room. I kept waiting for their outbursts, but none came.

I sat on the back deck, knowing how much I should enjoy it.

We'd had a heavy ocean storm the night before. The surf was high now, but the stormclouds had flown eastward, leaving the coast bathed in sun and springtime. Blackbirds and jays were having a field day because the leaves and ground were wet; their songs resounded through the little canyon before me. And to my right, gulls sang in the surfline, fishing and playing as usual.

It should have felt idyllic.

My problem was not my work — which was strewn around both the outdoor deck and "my" chair in the living room. Yes, it was a Sunday morning, a day when I "should" be resting. But these were the final-final galleys of the text of this book, and the last corrections had to be made in order to get the book printed on schedule.

Something was gnawing at me, hard and relentless. I was feeling — what was it?

incomplete

That was it. But why? Just what was "incomplete?" I got more coffee, sat back down.

The knowing crept up on me until I couldn't hold my eyes open. Soon I felt as if I had sand in them, as if I were "gritting my eyes."

your own work on anger

That was it. Here I was, editing a book on Anger Therapy. I'd read the manuscript a year or more earlier. Since then, I'd edited it, analyzed it, felt it, massaged it, worried over it like a doting parent. I'd dealt with its contents, its implications, its publishing, its design, its cover, even its promotion planning. And all the while, I'd had that slightly incomplete feeling about it.

During the previous months, I'd made several trips to introduce my own book, "Coincidences," around the country. People had been asking about the choice of titles for my book, and I'd responded — often on radio or TV — that "we all have have 'coincidences' in our lives, those seemingly unconnected events which we know just couldn't be unconnected." I'd explained so many times how these 'coincidences', when noticed, could be seized-upon and utilized — they were not really coincidental or unrelated, but rather invisible "miracles," opportunities.

And now, here I sat, editing a book on anger when, in fact, I hadn't finished working on the anger I felt within me.

I went back to the first chapter and re-read the text for my own personal use. I used the exercises: How had

I handled my own anger in the last few days or weeks? Had I been too "nice," suppressing my feelings again? What did my reactions say about my progress, or lack of progress?

I looked back at my life and re-realized what the suppression of anger had done.

I am an alcoholic. It had been more than 10 years since I began my recovery — a day-at-a-time process of progress, not perfection. Alcohol had been an emotional suppressant. Recovery meant dealing with my emotions.

> *another 'coincidence' —*
> *editing a book*
> *about anger,*
> *about running from it,*
> *about the self-destruction*
> *others have experienced*
> *from burying their anger.*

The children interrupted my thought. My son Huntley wanted to use my pens, sit at my desk to draw pictures. Jessie said she was going outside to ride her scooter, and wondered how soon we'd have breakfast.

As they hurried off to their new preoccupations, I returned to mine. I just couldn't ignore it now. Not because a book was coming out. Not because I, as the editor, "should" be free of the problems described in the book. No.

I wondered how much the Keyboard Effect (Chapter 1) had damaged my ability to enjoy life. Had the desire to suppres anger played a part in my old need to anesthetize my feelings with the booze? Had it played a part in my marital problems? And was it still causing me problems?

ohgawd Yes.

I went in to the den, found my address book, and thought maybe I'd call Roger Daldrup down in Tucson. I'd be going through Arizona on a business trip the coming week. Maybe I could take an extra day and do some personal work with him . . .

There are breakthrough moments in our lives. But they are rare. The more common experience is simple progress. I should be content with little steps, and thinking of Roger Daldrup that Sunday morning was just one more step. But I didn't need to see him — I had the book and its method right in my hands.

I will not wake up some morning knowing I have achieved emotional and spiritual perfection, that I've finally Made It.

> *But do I know that?*
> *Or do I still get those irrational moments*
> *when I think I'll*
> *get perfect*
> *in a single instant?*

Even in the last week of editing this text, I was still using the book personally. Its step-by-step, chapter-by-chapter approach was just what I needed. And I felt that so many of the people I've known could use it, too. It felt wonderful, knowing that.

— SCOTT B. SMITH

ABOUT THE
ANGER THERAPIST

Roger J. Daldrup, Ph.D., is a Tucson psychologist. Since 1962, he has been a member of the University of Arizona faculty where he is a professor of counseling and guidance.

He has also been engaged in private practice and has worked with thousands of men and women over the past 20 years. Dr. Daldrup has conducted hundreds of workshops at the U of A and for other organizations, as well as workshops and therapy retreats for singles, couples and groups in Arizona and, by invitation, in other states.

Many other psychologists, social workers and counselors have been trained by him in the specialized discipline of Anger Therapy. In recent years, he has responded to invitations to conduct these training workshops at universities in Hawaii, England, Belgium and Greece and has been invited to return to these countries and to Ireland.

Dr. Daldrup believes that psychotherapy as a purely verbal endeavor has long since reached its limits. Therefore, Anger Therapy emphasizes "experiencing" in contrast to talking about the experience; it is based on doing, rather than discussing — on taking action rather than analyzing.

For the past several years, he has been involved in clinical research on the relationship of anger to pain and disease, the preliminary results of which appear for the first time in lay language in this book. He has also commenced work on a three-year study of the results of anger release on Adult Children of Alcoholics. Over the years, he has also done continuing work with women who suffer from relationship addiction.

Anger Therapy is a vital, developing arena, and three of Dr. Daldrup's graduate students have earned their Ph.D. degrees with dissertations written on aspects of his Anger Therapy.

The specific anger exercises, which appear at the ends of chapters, were developed from his clinical experience.

ABOUT THE WRITER

Award-winning writer Dodie Gust has had a varied career that includes newspapers — reporting, photography, editing and being editor-publisher of an arts/culture newspaper of her own for five years — magazine article, booklet and book writing, and public information program direction and development for state agencies, universities and private corporations.

Most recently, she was a feature writer on psychology, ethics and values, as well as religion editor, for the Arizona Daily Star in Tucson, a job from which she resigned to devote full time to book writing plus anger-management workshops and training.

She first met Roger Daldrup in 1972 when she was an Information Specialist in the University of Arizona News Bureau. The first of several stories she has written on his therapy appeared in Arizona Magazine that year.

In the tradition of in-depth journalistic reporting, she participated in several group therapy sessions to add the first-hand dimension to the story. Nine years later, when an old anger, long thought dead and buried, flared up, she contacted Dr. Daldrup for help.

The completion of that long-standing, mostly hidden but still-stored anger in just three short sessions convinced her it was time to share this simple, effective action therapy with a wider segment of the public. The exercises and other tools of the Anger Therapy release methods learned in the process of writing this book and in several years of further study were all incorporated, with extremely positive results, into her own program of growth.

She now lives in Seattle, where she teaches anger management.

1

ANGER

Anger is powerful. It's been the driving force behind some of the most destructive acts in human history.

Anger is also unpredictable; we never know quite when it is going to erupt, in ourselves or others.

No wonder we have an almost inbred fear of anger.

But, in and of itself, anger is not something to be feared or hated. It is simply one of the basic human emotions — along with love, grief, joy, surprise, yearning, impatience, enthusiasm and many others.

Emotions are simply feelings, and it is our feelings and the way they are balanced within our psyches and personalities that tip our personal scale of happiness and unhappiness, even of health and illness.

We begin by accepting the fact that the emotions are neither good nor bad. It is what we do with them — how we express them or don't express them — that makes them negative or positive.

To better understand anger, let's look at some of its characteristics.

One dictionary defines it as a strong passion or emotion of displeasure — and usually antagonism — that is excited by a sense of injury or insult.

In other words, there is usually an element of hurt involved in anger. Injury and anger are two sides of the same emotional coin: We seldom feel angry without also feeling hurt (insulted, injured) to some degree, and we seldom experience hurt without feeling anger (displeasure, irritation, antagonism) at the cause of the pain. Sometimes, it's just the threat of being hurt which triggers anger.

Another dictionary definition calls anger a strong surge of feeling marked by an impulse to outward expression, and often accompanied by complex bodily reactions.

Anger's impulse to express itself is so inherent and so insistent that if we do not voluntarily express it in healthy, productive ways, the emotional system itself will make endless attempts to express it in any way it can, sometimes with destructive and painful results.

The healthy, productive methods for expressing anger without hurting ourselves or others do exist. They go beyond intellectual insights about anger and help us express it in a way that truly "completes" it, thus ridding the system of its negative effects.

Learning to use the specific techniques that are explained in both the text and the exercises is the precise purpose of this book.

Through use and practice of these techniques, you can satisfy the system's need to express anger — but in productive ways that permit a positive release of energy.

The productive techniques explained in this book are obviously quite different from some of the commonly used methods — screaming out accusations, heaping blame, causing a public scene, withholding love, playing martyr, using up our time, energy and peace of mind on revenge or "going to war" with another person. These negative methods can be damaging to the emotional and physical well being of ourselves and others. They are also ineffective; they don't get rid of the anger.

Let's explore some of the subtle, counterproductive methods for expressing anger that are frequently used in our culture.

Non-Directed Anger

Non-focused, non-directed expression of anger — "taking it out" on whatever or whoever is handy — isn't effective.

This method of expressing is the classic kicking-the-cat-because-you're-angry-at-your-spouse maneuver. One woman client told of deliberately breaking her favorite collector jazz records in the heat of an argument with her new husband, punctuating her yelled litany of grievances with the breaking of the records, one by one. She let off some of the steam of the moment but the next day the anger was still there — and her records were in the trash can.

One man "beat up" his Mercedes when his girlfriend broke a date with him. It didn't do a thing for the romance or his anger and frustration but it left him without transportation for a week and put a sizeable dent in his savings account.

Stuffing Anger

Another widespread way of dealing with anger — another way that doesn't work — is suppression.

Suppression or stuffing the emotion (pushing it down in the system, burying it, masking it with other emotions or with indifference) doesn't complete the anger and in fact, it puts the whole emotional system in a state of suppression.

Our emotions don't operate independently of each other any more than our organs function in isolation from each other. When the heart is not functioning properly, the lungs quickly get in trouble too. Similarly, when we suppress one emotion, we suppress them all to some extent.

The Keyboard Effect

We call this the keyboard effect because it is analagous to pressing the soft pedal of a piano — which mutes all the notes of the keyboard, the high notes as well as the low notes.

Similarly, when we press down the pedal on the emotional keyboard to suppress anger, we automatically suppress love, joy and other emotions at the same time.

The price we pay for soft-pedaling the emotional system is that we cannot fully enjoy a sunrise, allow closeness, become truly involved with another person or experience pleasant feelings of any kind to the fullest degree.

The energy required to suppress and store anger also makes us feel more tired with each passing year; we feel run down, turned-off, discouraged. This is why we experience a return of positive energy when we complete anger properly.

Stuffed anger is not anger that's been eliminated. At a conscious level, we may think it's gone, until something — a TV scene, a forgotten phrase, a song, a tone of voice, a look-alike face — triggers the memory of an incident that was the source of that particular stored anger. When this happens, we experience that old anger in full force, as if the incident that precipitated it were happening right now. Once again, we feel the anger pounding through the bloodstream and dominating our minds — until we manage to push it down again.

The Angry Filter

These stored-up feelings become a filter between us and the world, a filter through which everything coming in or going out of our emotional system must pass.

An angry filter may color our world as a cold and unfriendly place. Since our filter makes the incoming messages seem hostile, we often respond by thinking we had better be careful and keep our guard up; we are fearful of letting others know how we feel or who we really are because they may take advantage of us.

The same filter also distorts our outgoing messages. We may want to be loving and supportive and encouraging to others but these attempts are frequently discolored by the angry filter. A husband who says to his wife, "Of course I love you, dammit; what's the matter?" may be trying to express love to her but she receives the real message — his anger. If he could learn to complete his anger, his expression of love would come through clean and clear, not clouded by the filter.

The too-common attempt to experience only the emotions that fall within a designated acceptable range means that we are treating one part of the emotional system as less important or more dangerous than another. This suppression actually puts our system in a state of imbalance — and it never works.

Anger Will Out

When anger is buried, its need for expression manifests in other ways. A resentment may eat holes in our stomachs to create ulcers or shoot holes in our logic to wreak mental havoc. In some cases, the anger transmutes to another emotion so that it appears in the form of fear, guilt or depression. In severe cases, the anger may vent itself in abuse of self or others.

One way or another, anger will out.

This has now been verified by scientific and empirical studies done by many social and medical scientists. Almost daily, new evidence is reported in the growing body of literature and research data that confirms the negative effects of anger on the body, mind and spirit.

The simple Anger Therapy techniques used by the people you will meet in this book and by countless others can be used by you in your own home. The information and exercises give you the tools for finishing or completing anger in order to rid the system of negative effects.

Peace, freedom, enjoyment, confidence and vitality are among the rewards we start experiencing in our lives as we move from faulty expression or suppression to completion and release. This book shows how to make that move.

(As with all emotional problems, you may need professional counseling. This book and the techniques are not meant to be a substitute.)

EXERCISES

Exercises can be done at any time — and repeated as desired — but the sooner they are begun, the sooner the rewards are experienced. Completing the exercises as you go along also allows you to relate to the material that follows in a more personal way.

Exercise 1. The Imprint Exercise.

The purpose of this exercise is to imprint on your mind and allow your system to internalize an important underlying principle of this self-help course — that the reason for expressing anger is to free yourself of its negative effects.

Several times a day for the next few days, repeat the following sentence to yourself:

"The reason for expressing anger is to rid myself of its poison."

Exercise 2. Identifying One Method of
Dealing With Anger.

What was your method of expressing or suppressing the last time you got angry? Be specific (preferably in writing) in describing both the event and your responses. Tell exactly how you handled the anger, and describe how you felt afterward. The point here is just to see how you react.

2

CHOOSING ANGER
RESPONSES

Discovering how our individual anger responses were shaped is the first step toward being able to discard or change ineffective and counterproductive responses.

Parental Influences

Most of us learn our dominant responses to the world around us and to the emotions inside us at home. We start learning these ways to act and react when we are very young and most impressionable.

We start by copying the behavior of parents and other major models.

If Dad consistently becomes angry at Mother, the son can pick up the idea that men should become angry at women. If Mom expresses her irritation (a form of anger somewhat like a low-grade, sometimes chronic, infection of the emotional system) at Dad by carping at him, the daughter can see this as a legitimate way to express resentment.

One father may deal with his anger by yelling, another by being physically abusive, another by leaving the house. One mother may express anger by using the silent treatment, another by blaming or crying and still another by acting superior. (None of these behaviors is limited to either men or women; these are simply examples.)

Another reaction, learned in childhood, can be the holding-in caused by fear.

One woman who sought counseling said her mother constantly gave her the unspoken message: "Walk softly, your father can't handle it." The daughter, in dealing with her anger at her own husband, had added a word to the message: "He can't handle it now." She was married to a man who had been working for years on his Ph.D. degree. He kept changing his doctoral dissertation proposal and starting anew and she kept feeling, "I can't unload this on him now." She was "on hold" with her irritations and resentments for six years.

A husband whose wife had just been passed over for a promotion in her career fell into the same trap with his anger at her lack of interest and participation in a small hobby-turned-business-venture they had begun together. He told himself, "I can't burden her now; she's already upset."

If we were brought up to believe that expressing anger is "bad," we may decide to become stoics and never admit to having any; we develop a front of bravado or indifference. If we were trained to not cause a ruckus, we may express our anger by blame of others or as self-blame, which breeds guilt feelings.

Usually we follow parental models but sometimes we look at a parent's way of handling anger and reject it, deciding to respond in the opposite way.

One woman who described her mother as being "an angry, screaming, hysterical person" made the conscious decision: "I'm not going to be like her." She was careful not to raise her voice. In fact, she didn't admit even to herself that she ever became angry. The anger she had suppressed for years finally brought her to a bursting point.

As we make an effort to recall our formative years and look at our models from childhood it usually becomes evident that we have some characteristics from both parents or other major models.

These early choices about how we will deal with anger are hidden deep in the psyche and may be the cause of a multitude of unsolved problems and unresolved relationships 15 — or 55 — years later.

Societal Influences

Our responses to anger also are shaped by the society in which we live and participate.

One of the ways in which society convinces us that it is wrong or dangerous or impolite to verbalize personal frustration and injured feelings is by giving social sanction to a number of anger myths.

The most commonly perpetuated myth is that people who are "nice," "kind," "civilized," "educated," "sophisticated," don't get angry. This is ridiculous. No one is exempt from this basic human emotion. But, in our society, this myth is sometimes carried to such an extreme that people are afraid to disagree in conversation.

Another myth is, "Don't admit it and it will go away." An example of trying to live up to this myth is the man or woman who — after a stressful confrontation at work in which angry feelings at bosses or co-workers were stifled — goes home to the lovely suburban house, has dinner, tucks the kids into bed, walks the dog, goes to bed and has intercourse (it can't be called making love) and, all the time, is boiling inside.

Another myth is that "anger and love don't mix." It is true that they are separate feelings, but it's illogical to think we are not supposed to get angry at the person we love. The deeper the caring, the deeper the hurt and anger.

A related myth says that "expressing displeasure or disagreement puts a relationship at risk." It would be more accurate to say that relationships in which there is little else but nods of agreement die very quickly. We believe that if a monitoring device could be hooked up to one of these alliances it would register a dead relationship — one that never beeps, blurps or changes, and never goes anywhere.

A true relationship takes many forms and directions. It is not all loving, not all angry, not all joyful, not all sad, not all anything.

One myth that currently permeates our culture — and, unfortunately, even some counseling communities — is that expressing anger breeds more anger, leading to lack of control. In following chapters, we will present case histories and research data that clearly refute this contention and show that when anger is properly expressed it is completed and processed out of the system.

For now, one example from a case history will illustrate the point. This man said, "I'm afraid I'll kill somebody if I express my anger."

He was partly right. This particular man had an extreme degree of anger; he also had a volatile personality; and he had previously acted out his angers in destructive ways. He *was* in danger of hurting or killing someone — if he didn't get his anger out, express it in a productive way.

In therapy, he was encouraged to own up to the feeling of wanting to kill — without killing. He released the uncontrollable element in a safe environment rather than out in society.

By choosing to express his rage through directed Anger Therapy techniques that combined physical as well as verbal release methods (which will be fully explained as we proceed in the course), he didn't have to risk really hurting another. He "went through" his perceived need to attack or kill, completed the anger and was freed of it.

The depth of this man's long-standing fury required help from a trained Anger Therapy facilitator, but individuals with modified forms of the same feelings can usually deal with the anger successfully through the exercises that focus on techniques of completion and release.

We have named only a few of the myths regarding anger that, along with parental modeling, influence us when we choose our anger responses.

At some point in our lives, we decided, probably subconsciously, what our own anger responses were going to be. We continue to use these methods until we make a conscious decision to change them.

The exercises allow us to identify the roots of our own specific responses.

EXERCISES

Exercise 1. The Trip Back Home (Discovering how parents dealt with anger).

Relax. Close your eyes. Take a trip down memory lane to the house in which you grew up. See your mother and father or other major caretaker there. Get them in good focus. Where are they and what are they doing?

Now, remember how they responded to various things. First, remember how each of them expressed caring, love, affection. Next, remember how each expressed fear, concern, worry. Recall how they expressed joy, excitement, happiness. Lastly, remember how each expressed anger, resentment and hostility — especially toward you.

As you remember these things, notice what decision you made regarding the expression of feelings, especially anger and hurt. Try to put your decision in one sentence, such as, "I decided that . . . (I would never be like him . . . crying is a good way to get out of unpleasant situations . . . I'd always just be 'nice' . . .)."

Now, mentally thank your mother and father for spending these remembered moments with you today and say goodbye to them in any way you please.

Return to your awareness in the here and now.

Write down the childhood decision you identified and keep this for future reference. Is that decision still in force today?

If you did not identify a decision, don't worry about it; you did make one and you will eventually recall it.

Exercise 2. Childhood Anger.

Remember a time when you got angry as a child. What brought it on? How did you respond and what were the consequences? Did you get yelled at? Punished? Or were you supported for your reaction at that time?

Is this where you started getting off-track in expressing anger? How do you feel as you remember this experience? Connect this memory to yourself today and to your present mode of dealing with anger.

Exercise 3. Identifying Your Anger Myths.

On a blank sheet of paper, write: "Anger is . . ." Then complete the sentence with as many different endings of thoughts, concepts, feelings, etc. which come to your mind (e.g., Anger is . . . not nice . . . dangerous . . . frightening . . .). When your mind goes blank, close your eyes for a few seconds and allow any new, additional thoughts to come. Do this until you have a complete listing of all the perceptions you hold regarding anger.

3

THE BLAMING GAME

The blaming game is an all-time favorite for dealing with anger. In this game, blaming masquerades as expressing. But it's not honest or true expression because blaming is not direct and straightforward; it is done *in place of* honestly expressing anger. The channel it offers to the system for anger release is in reality a maze.

Like other faulty ways of expressing, blaming is not successful in giving relief from anger's gnawing effects.

An example is the case of a woman named Elaine who had come for marriage counseling with her husband. She said, "I'm here because George has a problem. He doesn't express his feelings. He gives me a cold stare or looks right through me as if I'm not there; he goes off to his workshop when I try to discuss our relationship. He won't deal with anything, and it's ruining our marriage."

She added, "I've read about how we have to deal with anger and get it out; I deal with mine all the time."

As she started "dealing" with her anger in her accustomed way in therapy, it soon became evident that what she was doing was not "getting it out," but blaming.

In an exchange with George in the counseling session, her remarks followed this pattern: "You won't talk to me," "You never pay attention to me," and, "This is the poorest possible excuse for a marriage" (which carries the unspoken accusation that "it's all your fault"). The blaming statements continued at length.

Asked if she felt better after dealing with anger this way, Elaine voiced a frustrated, "No."

This same question has been proposed to hundreds of men and women in counseling sessions, anger workshops and Anger Therapy courses who acknowledged frequent use of the blaming mode. Not one has ever answered in the affirmative. Blaming provides no relief from anger.

Yet, this way of "dealing" is common. Some persons rely on it almost exclusively as a response to anger, and most of us resort to it at one time or another.

Blaming in Public

One reason blaming is so widespread is that it is more socially acceptable than some other ways of venting angry feelings. In fact, it is frequently done in public, sometimes in the form of complaining, a less confrontive way of blaming. Often, it is done with deviousness — in the transparent guise of a humorous remark, or with a "sweet" tone of voice, for example — but it is still blaming, and neither of these devices serves to mask the real meaning of the comments.

Other times, the blame is conveyed by "complimenting" someone else's behavior in a very pointed way: "Isn't that nice? He always pays attention to his wife at parties," or, "She really knows how to dress."

Getting Even

Blaming's popularity also relates to its use as a tool for "getting even." It's readily available when we want to strike out at someone whom we see as the cause of our frustration, irritation or unhappiness. Blaming is a retaliation that seeks to "pay back" unpleasant feelings.

The blaming game puts players in a no-win situation. It is unsatisfying because it never finishes the unfinished angers. Every time we use the blaming tactic, the game board or game screen directs us to "Begin Again."

Once the blaming mode is adopted, people easily get ensnared in its cyclic maze, often finding themselves stuck between hurt and anger and not able to express either effectively.

To get unstuck from this very uncomfortable position and get to "Home Free" or "Exit" on the game, we begin by changing our language.

Language is intimately involved in our expression or suppression of emotion.

Blaming Language

Blaming language is "You" language: "*You* don't pay as much attention to me as you do to . . .," "*You* flirt with other men," "*You* forgot my birthday," "*You* don't come with me when I give a public talk," "*You* don't keep the house as nice as so and so," "*You* never clean up the yard," "*You* don't have time to listen to me but you spend hours gossiping on the phone (or drinking beer with your friends)."

All of these statements really mean, "*I* am hurt or angry or both that you did or didn't do the thing at issue."

In the blaming game, words are also used improperly. The incorrect use of the word "why" is a prime example when it is used to ask questions that aren't really questions — "questions" that are not seeking answers.

The statement, "Why were you late?" probably means, "I am angry that you were late." The question, "Why did you do that?" really means, "I am hurt that you did that" or "Don't do that anymore."

These "questions" are ineffective because they don't give the real message, and both parties know this.

Blaming can be detected in the voice and facial expression as well as in language. It may come out as a high-pitched whine, as a sarcastic tone, or with a haughty or disgusted look.

George, for example, who retreated to his workshop when Elaine started her blaming, usually gave her a parting look that clearly said, "There you go again. Your nagging is too much; you are causing me to retreat to the only place in the house where there's peace and quiet."

His way of expressing anger (withdrawing plus using implied blame) was obviously no more effective than his wife's method.

Winning the Game

The objective of the anger exercises is to move from blaming to uncovering and releasing the underlying anger. When Elaine and George started communicating honestly with "I" language, expressing their feelings about situations rather than talking about the incidents, they began to get unstuck with their hurt and anger.

In some cases, the blaming we are doing in current relationships may relate to old angers carried over from previous relationships in which the anger is still unfinished. The system attempts to complete these unfinished angers with the person at hand.

Our anger work through the exercises and through practice in day-to-day living situations frees us from both old and more recent angers. This allows us to live life in the present tense.

Action is the foundation and strength of this Anger Therapy book for a very practical reason: Action is what works.

Excerpts from clients' case histories serve to illustrate the techniques and to give examples of their effectiveness, but you are your own best example. Words explain the self-help exercises but the results you personally achieve explain the dynamics of the therapy much more explicitly. **The only thing that will convince you that the exercises work is actually doing the exercises.**

Exercise No. 1 on the next page is your introduction to the important technique of expressing anger to a person *in absentia*. This method allows you to practice the techniques before using them in face-to-face expression, thus taking some of the "sting" out of the anger beforehand.

The exercise can also be used whenever you are not able to express an anger directly at the time for any one of a number of reasons — because of fear of the person, because the other person will not allow expression, because the individual lives elsewhere or is dead, or because you are just not yet able to do this.

EXERCISES

Exercise 1. Monitoring Your Language With a Tape Recorder.

Try this exercise in a room by yourself. Choose a person with whom you have unfinished anger (if angry or blaming thoughts occur to you whenever you think of the person, the anger has not been completed).

Turn on the recorder and then forget about it. Imagine that the person is in an empty chair facing yours (straight-backed chairs are suggested for this exercise). Place your feet firmly on the floor and act out a confrontation with the person. Speak to him or her the way you would like to speak if you could really tell the individual what you think about him or her. Tell the person how you feel about his or her actions during specific events in the past or in the current relationship.

Try to let yourself go; let yourself get into the expressing, not trying to control your language but saying the statements that come naturally to mind. Purposely let yourself use blame language if that is what wants to come out. Self-consciousness will pass in a few minutes if you persevere.

When finished, listen to the tape to monitor the type of language you used. If you used "You" language such as, "You ought to . . .," "You make me . . ." or "Why don't you . . .?" then you are in a blaming mode.

Now, mentally redo each of your sentences, using "I" language such as "I resent you for . . .," "I am angry at you for . . ." or "I am hurt at . . ."

Do you feel differences, physical and emotional, by changing the language?

Exercise 2. Monitoring Your Voice.

Again play the tape you have recorded, listening to the sound of your voice. Can you hear a high-pitched whine or an accusatory tone?

Using the mentally redone sentences from above, experiment with saying the "I" sentences out loud. Say them with force! Yelling and swearing are encouraged if this is what you feel like doing.

Tape record the experiment and compare the energetic message with the previous message. Which was more satisfying?

Exercise 3. Finding Your Blame Rationale.

Think of a situation in which you are still maintaining some anger. Notice if there are any thoughts of blaming or complaining and think about what would happen if you became angry about the situation instead. Act this out in your mind. How would you be different if you expressed anger directly instead of blaming or complaining? What would occur in your life if you did this?

The honest answers to these questions will give you insights into the reasons you have given yourself for blaming or complaining.

Exercise 4. Blaming Models.

Make another quick trip back home (see page 32) and remember how those around you used blaming and complaining as an anger response. You may want to write a list. Identify which of these people you most resemble and which you least resemble.

4

THE LOOK AND FEEL OF ANGER

We may not be able to reach out and touch it, but anger touches us very forcefully. We can feel another person's anger and we readily recognize its faces, postures, and sounds when we encounter them.

"You could just feel the tension in the room" is a statement commonly used to describe anger's tangibility.

Anger emits a specific kind of energy that seems to be coming out of the person's pores. It can fill a room, a whole house, with a certain vibration.

Anger also affects physical appearance. Facial expressions of anger are sometimes blatant and obvious — a frown, a scowl, a glare, a sneering, derisive or "hateful" look. At other times, the signs are less overt but still easily perceived — tightened lips, clenched jaws, gritted teeth, pallor of the skin or flushing of the cheeks and neck, a slight flaring of the nostrils.

These individual anger countenances differ from person to person. What is more uniform, more universal is the anger "aura" — a "blackness" or "dark cloud" over the face. The eyes lack clarity and there is also a darkness around them. The pupil appears cloudy and color fades.

Men and women who are carrying inordinate amounts of stored anger around with them on a continuing basis also have a tendency to manifest it in their grooming. One woman realized she had let her appearance "go to hell in a handbasket," as she described it. Men may seem to always need a shave; women may have lifeless looking hair. Clothes may be rumpled looking, or extremely dark and severe.

Or, chronically angry people may go to the other extreme, wearing flamboyant, garish clothing and adopting exaggerated hair styles.

There are many exceptions to this generalization, as there are to all generalizations, but among people undergoing Anger Therapy, these two extremes are frequently seen at the initiation of the therapy.

Other angry people are well-groomed from the chin up; they obviously give care to their skin and hair. These people are very attractive above the neck. Below the Adam's apple, they are a disaster area.

These are the women and men who store everything below their collar bones. If you know persons who fit this description, casually try to discover if they own a full-length mirror. Odds are high against it. These people usually won't have one in their houses or apartments — they don't want to see the full picture. They can look in the face mirror and receive the feedback that they are OK.

Posture, physical gestures, voice pitch and manner of speaking are also altered by anger held in storage. Physical characteristics of a person in Anger Therapy change as he or she moves, stage by stage, from denial and retention of anger to acceptance and healthy release.

Denial of Anger

At the initiation of directed Anger Therapy, the client frequently denies possessing anger.

One person may have a defiant swagger, another acts puzzled, still another may appear to be devoid of emotion. These are all efforts to not disturb the "calmness" or "okay-ness" they are trying to achieve — or which they have already reached by stifling their emotions.

One typical swaggerer had a denial "pitch" that went something like this: "I don't feel anything. It doesn't bother me that she left and took the kids and went off with someone else. It doesn't bother me; I'm better off without her."

The man was talking in a monotone that rendered the words lifeless. The emphasis was on the talking; he was still in the dead state, not yet in the feeling stage.

A woman in a similar situation buried her anger under haughty indifference. "I don't need him. What did he ever do for me anyway? I'm getting along just fine without him. Better. I'm not angry, I'm glad he's gone; I just wish he'd gone sooner, or that I had."

The woman's voice was also lifeless even though her words were defiant — coldly defiant, shooting out of her mouth like icicles that hung in the air.

Challenging Denial

In Anger Therapy, the therapist will often challenge these denial recitals by asking, "How much do you think you can tolerate before you do get upset? How much are you willing to stand before you get angry about it?"

The therapist asked the man, "What would it take to bother you? If her new boyfriend stranded her and she called to ask you to rescue her, would that bother you?"

Challenging the woman, the therapist said, "Would a phone call from your husband asking for money to bail him out of a scrape he got into with his girlfriend make you angry?"

This type of therapeutic challenge usually evokes a glimmer of recognition from the person that there is indeed something being held in emotional storage — something very disturbing.

When the swaggerer was challenged, he started to flush in the face and clench his jaws. He began to speak rapidly through gritted teeth, spitting out his words in clipped rounds like machine-gun fire.

In the session with the woman, she responded to the challenge by starting to cry.

Both started expressing, but still with reservations. This first recognition that there may be much that is pent-up inside — and the attendant implication that all this will have to be dealt with — can be quite fearful to the person. The subconscious reaction is apt to be: "What am I getting into?"

At this point, there is commonly a last-ditch effort to stay in the dead stage, to keep the emotions locked in.

The Implosive Stage

In this implosive or holding-in stage, there is an internal conflict because the anger that has been temporarily deadened by denial wants to burst into flame to express itself while the conscious mind is trying to quell the fire, fearing the combustion.

The implosive stage precedes the explosive stage, both in therapy and in one-to-one encounters in daily life. In therapy, it precedes acceptance of the anger and the beginning of anger work in which the anger can "explode" in a controlled exercise.

In personal encounters, it also comes before the explosive or letting-out stage. Here, the letting out may be productive or counterproductive, depending on the method selected for expression.

Some people in the implosive stage become pale, perspire lightly, sit in a tight and tense position, sometimes with their hands between their knees. There are frequently changes in breathing and blood pressure.

One woman while in this stage, was talking in a faint, weak drone. There was no energy in her voice and she was sitting in a hunched-over position. She had removed her shoes and kept digging her toes into the rug, clawing the rug with them while repeating such statements as, "I'm not angry; he was so good to me most of the time."

A person in therapy or confrontation who is clasping his or her hands together or who is standing in a pigeon-toed or knock-kneed position may well be in the implosive stage. The pigeon-toed or knock-kneed stance usually signifies the child cowering before the "big" adult.

When the person moves past this and starts getting into the anger, the back straightens, the chest comes out, the shoulders go back, and the body posture becomes erect with body weight distributed to both feet.

As the anger is processed productively and released, the words and gestures start coming in flowing motions rather than in jerks and twitches; the eyes become clear, the frown lines smooth out. The person appears much more attractive, the "aura" is light and the energy he or she gives off becomes nourishing rather than toxic to other people.

EXERCISES

Exercise 1. Your Last Anger.

Find a quiet place to sit or lie down. Notice your breathing. Allow your breath to come in fully and to go out completely. Do this several times. Now, allow your breathing to fall into its normal pattern and remember the last time you were really angry.

Where were you? What were the circumstances? Who was there? Remember what led up to the anger. How were you feeling as the anger developed inside you?

Notice what the other person was doing. How did you respond? How did it feel to respond that way?

Now, come back to awareness of where you are now and look back at this experience. What were your feelings and your physical responses as you remembered the different scenes in this incident? Did you respond with a feeling of tension in the stomach, head, shoulders? Did you have a dry mouth, a tightening of the jaws or a general feeling of anxiety? Did you remember sounds and smells?

The symptoms you experience as you remember this situation will give you an indication of whether or not this is an anger that needs to be worked on.

Exercise 2. Working It Out.

When the above-recalled experience occurred, were you left feeling satisfied when it ended? If so, what accounted for your satisfaction?

If you did not feel satisfied, think of what you would like to do differently if you could re-do the situation.

Go to the fantasy situation and imagine doing it this new way. Compare the results. If you do sense some change in the way you feel after re-doing the incident, you are beginning to understand how unfinished angers from the recent or distant past can be finished in the present.

If you did not experience a sense of relief, this situation needs more work. Long-stored angers sometimes require intense application of several exercises.

Exercise 3. Mirror Exercise.

Sit in front of a full-length mirror. Express some recent or lingering angers silently. Notice your facial expressions and body posture.

Stand up in front of the mirror, and express the anger out loud. Check out the position of feet, arms, hands. If your shoulders are rounded, throw them back and try again. If your body is slouching, straighten the backbone and repeat the exercise. Keep feet solidly planted on the floor.

Evaluate the difference in the way you feel after re-doing the exercise with assertion.

5

ANGER ON MY MIND

Anger plays tricks on our minds.

Logic, for instance, takes flight when anger rushes in. A lot of anger just doesn't make sense.

We may think our angers make sense, or that they should, but is this a reasonable expectation?

There is some basis for expecting thoughts to be logical; that is their domain. But feelings operate in a different sphere and, when there is a contest between emotion and rationality, emotion usually wins.

English writer Alexander Pope acknowledged this fact of life more than 200 years ago when he wrote, "The ruling passion, be it what it will/The ruling passion conquers reason still."

Emotion Rules Reason

The often illogical behavior of human beings when they are in a state of infatuation provides a lively demonstration of the poet's truth.

And, it's not only in romantic love situations that emotion clouds reason. When anger is the emotion that's on the front burner, rationality often goes up in smoke.

Consider the case of Janet, a 50-year-old who was carrying around old anger at her mother for not sending her to college.

Janet was acutely aware of and grateful for an abundance of gifts from her mother: the instilling of personal integrity, honesty, manners, good habits of health and hygiene, respect for language and grammar, love of books and appreciation of the arts. This, plus a lifetime of personal, nonjudgmental love.

Janet said she had long since come to understand that her mother — who had had only an eighth-grade education herself but who always pursued self-education — had been extremely conscientious in passing on her hard-won knowledge and skills.

"She was also important as a role model because she did very well — without education and in a pre-equal-rights era — in a career in the judicial court system," said Janet.

"Logically, I shouldn't feel hurt and anger about what she didn't do for me. She gave me much more than she herself had had. The recurring thoughts of blame make me feel so unappreciative of all the rest. This is so unreasonable of me, so petty.

"I wish it would go away and, most of the time, I think it's gone. Then something reminds me that I don't have a college degree, even though I've had a very successful career, and I want to blame her. The resentment is still there and it rankles."

Feelings such as Janet's are not rare. Understanding that her feelings were unreasonable didn't serve to erase the blame impulse.

Whether or not the feelings are logical is not the point. What is important is acknowledging that they exist, that we have them and that we are the ones who have to contend with them.

Contending means making a choice between trying to suppress them or completing and being freed of

them. Janet had been trying suppression — unsuccess-
fully — for more than three decades. She had also tried
to analyze the anger away.

Neither suppressing the anger nor analyzing it
brings release. Will power and brainpower usually lose
in the face of strong emotion. The emotion keeps sabo-
taging our perception until the mind stops long enough
for us to take care of the feelings.

Janet made the decision to complete the anger. But
she was understandably reluctant to express it in person to her 73-year-old mother, whom she loved deeply
and did not want to hurt.

Instead, she used one of the *in absentia* anger exercises designed for use when it is impossible or inadvis-
able — because of separation or other reasons — to
personally confront.

On her own, following the instructions, she was able
to finish off this old anger once and for all.

She later said, "Once I expressed the anger out loud,
really loud, 'face-to-face,' and pounded it out at the
same time (see Exercise 1, page 60), the anger just
dissipated. It disappeared; there was almost a physical
sense of its leaving."

Janet hesitated a moment, a slightly puzzled expression on her face, and then continued: "That evening, a funny thing happened. I suddenly recalled something I had apparently blocked from memory for
30-some years.

"I was able to admit to myself that I had had the
opportunity to go to college. My grandmother had
wanted to send me to a very good all-girls' school. I
declined because I wanted a co-ed college or nothing. I
got nothing."

A couple years later, when Janet called to say hello,
she provided a postscript. She said she had been taking
evening college courses and had completed a dozen,
which expanded her career horizons and led to a job

change that offered more personal fulfillment. "Once I stopped blaming my mother and took responsibility myself, I had to make a choice about what I wanted to do about it," she said happily.

Instances of anger less logical than Janet's are legion. Here are a few examples. Have you ever felt:

— rage at the person who took the parking spot you had mentally claimed as yours;
— resentment at your partner when the TV was turned to the wrong station when you were planning to watch something else (which you didn't mention);
— jealous anger at a co-worker who was noticed for good work;
— rancor at a friend who called at an inopportune time;
— rancor at the same friend who didn't call when you were feeling lonely?

Mentally inventory your angers or resentments of the last few days. Are they logical? If they are like some of ours, comical would probably be a more accurate description, at least in retrospect.

Many angers, of course, are logical. It's perfectly logical to be angry when:

— your feelings are hurt,
— you've been used, manipulated, rejected, abused, harmed in any way,
— someone heaps you with blame,
— someone frightens you,
— you are verbally attacked or ridiculed.

These are but a few examples from hundreds of possible reasons for logical anger. But the thing to remember is that anger doesn't have to be logical to exist as anger.

Logical or illogical, if we do not purge the anger, it *will* affect our logic until we clear it out, influencing our thinking and decision making in the days and years to come.

Divorce Logic

Decisions in a divorce offer a typical example. Most people still have unfinished anger when the divorce decision is made. In fact, they have usually made the decision because an accumulation of anger and hurt convinces them that the only way to escape the pain of the relationship is to separate.

After the divorce, the pain is still there. The divorce provides the legal sanction for the physical severance but the psychological hooks are still intact. In an overwhelming number of cases, the decision to end a marriage emerges from an angry stance. The hooks the man and woman have in each other are composed of the unfinished business between them.

Since they are not yet complete with the relationship, one or both may be prone to giving the marriage another (ill-fated) try ("Maybe we ought to get back together").

Another couple may keep the marital battleground active after the divorce by continuing to rehash old conflicts or by using the children, the property settlement, tax returns or mutual friends to keep alive old conflicts and create new ones.

Before, not after, the decision is made to divorce or to remain together is the time to complete the unfinished business so that a rational decision can be made.

One client, an accountant who was conscious of the value of well-balanced books, asked his wife to accompany him to counseling sessions, even though they had made an irrevocable decision to divorce. She had originally objected, saying, "What's the point; we're getting divorced anyway."

The husband insisted, "We're going to balance the books before we make the split." His professional background and his common sense told him to add up the columns and reconcile the figures before closing the file.

The wife agreed to the counseling and, as a result, they both completed their angers and achieved an emotional "closure" of the relationship. They were able to go on to new phases of their lives with a set of clean, closed books behind them.

Unless the books are balanced, those carry-over debit figures from the old relationship can appear as opening entries in the ledger of a new relationship. When this happens, a relationship starts out in the red.

Half-Finished Anger

In a different situation involving uncompleted anger, a university student had worked out part of his anger in therapy but, a year later, the part still in storage began to cause him problems.

Originally, Paul came to counseling at the urging of his parents who were alarmed that he was "destroying his life." He was a talented artist but he had dropped out of college, and was experimenting with drugs.

His appearance and demeanor were slovenly and sullen.

At the end of the Anger Therapy sessions, in which he had been able to identify and release a great deal of pent-up anger at his father, Paul's life did turn around dramatically. He went back to college, was in the commercial art program at a state university, and had also completed two freelance projects for a large corporation.

Having successfully cleaned up his act and having proved himself "commercially," as he described it, he wanted to switch his degree program to fine art. This was his real interest but it was a vocational preference his father always branded as "totally impractical."

Home for the holidays at semester break, Paul himself called to set up a session.

"I've been working on a large oil painting," he said, "and it's going great. But, right in the middle of a brush stroke, I sometimes blank out. My mind just goes blank, for how long I don't know, and when I snap back I'm disoriented and full of anxiety.

"I'm not on drugs, I'm clean; I don't know what's the matter. Am I losing my mind?"

What soon came to the surface was that although Paul had previously released enough of the anger at his father to give him enough relief to allow him to make strides with his life, the process was not complete.

He was literally shutting off his mind to avoid the pain of that unfinished anger which began to surface again when he wanted to change to his chosen career field.

In an anger work-out session, he "seated" his father on a huge ottoman and stood in front of it with a bataca (a stuffed, bat-shaped "beating" device). He began to yell out his anger to his father, beating on the ottoman at the same time with all his strength.

"I've spent a year living up to your expectations and I'm angry at you for laying those expectations on me. I'm damn mad at you for expecting me to do what you want me to do — make a lot of money.

"I resent it that you don't care about what I want to do and I'm hurt that you don't trust me enough or respect me enough to let me make my own decisions about this. I'm damn mad at you for this!"

After he had done this for 20 or 30 minutes, naming specific incidents, he paused.

Paul took a deep breath and continued, "I'm grown up. I'm going to choose the career I want, and I don't give a damn if you like it or not. It's my life." He finished with one last strong wham of the bataca on the ottoman, heaved a big sigh and smiled.

The therapist asked him, "Can you go home now and tell that to your father in person?"

"Yes," said Paul.

He later reported that he'd been able to do just that, making the announcement to his father in a firm way, but without rancor (which he'd released in the explosive therapy session).

When Paul was able to discard the introjected values from his father and choose and embrace his own, he was able to switch degree programs without anger, guilt or anxiety.

He no longer "blanks out" when painting.

Introjected Values

Paul's case illustrates an important factor in dealing with anger — "introjection." He had introjected his father's values, taken them on as his own.

As noted earlier, we are all fed many values in childhood and we adopt them because they give us necessary guidelines for acting and reacting in society. But these introjected values may not be ours; we didn't consciously choose them and, when we are mature enough, we need to choose our own value system.

Paul, like many people, didn't know how to do this in a healthy way. At first, when he was in his mid and late teens, he rebelled against his parents and society. The past year in college, he had tried conforming to his father's values but that didn't work well either. Values taken on for fear of displeasing others are hard to live up to and they also create discomfort and anger because we are not being true to ourselves. Part of maturing is choosing our own standards and goals.

This does not mean that our values and beliefs are necessarily going to be different from those of our parents. Consciously making a decision to choose them, whatever they are, and claiming them as our own is what is important. When we do this we eliminate one probable source of anger from our lives.

Concentration

Locked-in anger can also scuttle the mind's power of concentration. One student who had breezed through high school and junior college suddenly faltered when he entered an out-of-state university.

He sought counseling, saying, "I can't concentrate; I can't remember what I study. I'm afraid I'm losing my brain power."

This student wasn't losing his brain power. His system was on overload with suppressed emotion, much of it anger at a series of ex-girl friends, and this was actually "weighing" on his mind, bogging it down.

He said he had "always had trouble with girls." But he didn't realize he was angry about this. Recalling the last brush-off, he said, "No, I don't feel bad about it. I knew she was in love with this other guy. Her thing with me was just sort of a moonlighting episode."

It was in group therapy with other students who met weekly that he acknowledged he was angry and hurt and felt used. His confidence was badly shattered from a string of unsuccessful attempts at relationships and the untended anger was drawing his attention away from his studies.

He'd been able to override the feelings previously but now, with the added stress of a demanding university program, his mind bogged down.

The solution was no different for this student than it was for the other people we have discussed: Admit the anger, work it out productively, be freed of it.

EXERCISES

Exercise 1. Pound It Out.

Decide what anger you wish to work on now. Imagine the person seated facing you from a couch, bed,
large ottoman, wood pile, or any other object that's
suitable both for a person (the source of your anger) to
sit on and for you to beat upon. Have ready a stick,
broom, rolled up newspaper, or a bataca (a bat-like
stuffed "beating" device used in Anger Therapy
sessions).

Stand facing the person you have mentally placed in
front of you and tell him or her: "I have asked you
here because I want to express my feelings to you."

Begin expressing your anger directly to the imaged
person, hitting the bed or whatever with your beater at
the same time.

Use "I" language to express your anger, resentment,
blame, hurt or whatever wants to come out. Be forceful in your language and voice and forceful in hitting
the bed.

Do this until your system tells you that you are
finished with the exercise for the time being. But continue it for at least 15 minutes, preferably longer.

When you stop, bid the person goodbye. "Thank you
for being with me today. I may call you back again.
Goodbye."

Exercise 2. Stand-and-Step Exercise.

This exercise is an analogy that illustrates how unfinished anger works in our system:

Stand. Start to take a step forward, but stop with your foot in mid-air. Stay that way. How comfortable does that feel?

With anger, many of us start to take the step forward with expression but stop in mid-air, so to speak.

If we keep our (anger) foot in mid-air, we learn to adjust to this; we start hopping around on one foot. One leg starts to atrophy. The other, in compensation, develops out of proportion. Soon, we convince ourselves this hopping on one leg is a normal way of ambulating.

We eventually give up the idea that we want to put our foot down and complete ourselves. If someone asks us why we are hopping around on one foot, we are surprised. We reply, "I always do it this way."

A person who accepts hopping around on one leg as normal behavior is also likely to have relationships with other hoppers. The hope is that the two suspended legs will balance each other so the two people can hop around together.

Now, repeat the stand-and-step exercise once more. This time stay in mid-air only for the count of three. Then let yourself go ahead and complete the step. How does that feel?

Exercise 3. Introjection Test.

Make a list of 10 basic beliefs you hold. In a facing column, list the important people in your life (parents, teachers, etc.) who hold the same beliefs. Examples of beliefs which might fit here are: "Earning a lot of money is necessary to be a success," "A democratic republic is the best system of government," "God loves me." Determine whether the values are yours or whether they belong to the people in the right hand column. Decide which ones you elect to keep and which you want to change.

6

ANGRY SEX

Suppressed anger has a profound negative effect on sexual intimacy. Stored anger causes "angry sex" that manifests in infrequent or disappointing lovemaking and, in more severe cases, in impotence, frigidity or premature ejaculation.

This is not too difficult to understand if we recall the earlier discussion about the "keyboard effect": Suppress one emotion and you suppress them all.

Constant Sex

Occasionally, a couple with unfinished anger at each other will use sex as an avoidance technique, resorting to it constantly — sometimes to the point of chronic physical and emotional fatigue — as a way to avoid dealing with angry feelings.

They use physical aggression in sex as a substitute for the emotional aggression (anger) they feel toward each other. Their subconscious rationale for constant sex is: "If we had good sex last night, today is going to be OK."

A couple may arrive for counseling with their repressed mutual anger so intense it can be felt and observed — yet insisting that "our sex life is still good." When a claim such as this co-exists with apparent anger, they are probably lying about their sex life or they are misperceiving it. It is likely not nearly as satisfactory emotionally as they say or think it is.

Although anger is sometimes avoided with constant "unfeeling" sex — detached, and "physical" versus sensual and loving — it more commonly causes partners to "distance" themselves from each other.

Distancing

The distancing begins with their refusal to address their angers. Anger has to be processed out of the system on a continuing basis or it grows in quantity until it has no place to go but into storage.

This is when the sexual suppression usually starts. One or both parties start physically distancing and there is less and less emotional and physical touching.

As this kind of physical drift between the partners becomes ever more obvious, they may try to "fix" the relationship with one of any number of emergency measures.

The Fixit Trip

The fixit trip is one such measure. One man and his wife who realized they were beginning to "get out of sync," decided to go away to a romantic vacation spot in Mexico and get back in synchronization in one week.

There was pleasant excitement about getting away and a tantalizing illusion that the trip was, somehow, magically, going to restore them to an idyllic matrimonial state. The setting was right: palm trees, beach, shops and scenic settings to explore. They shared their enjoyment of these explorations but they still weren't exploring personal issues.

At bedtime, the touching was tentative and cautious. The coupling was nonverbal; they went through the motions almost without emotion, as if replaying a scene from their own past — without sound, without color, without special effects. The sex was hardly satisfactory but they attributed this to the fact that they hadn't been away from home long enough. They were sure it would be "better tomorrow."

The situation back home — the children, the jobs, the responsibilities, all the things they had used as distractions to avoid communication and lovemaking — were now removed.

In Mexico, the palms continued to wave in the sea breeze, the candles still burned on the table at their "romantic" dinners under soft lights, and the music continued to play.

But, while these things work well as enhancements, they don't work well as replacements. The soft music, for instance, could have been an aid to letting feelings flow easily between them, but they weren't relaxed enough to allow that. The mariachi music didn't help either; it grated on their nerves because it was happy music and didn't appeal to them in their down state. They were depressed because the sex hadn't gotten "better tomorrow." The husband felt sexually inadequate and the wife felt undesirable.

Their fixit trip didn't work because they had not been taking care of the relationship on a day-to-day basis by dealing with their upsetness with each other as it occurred. They hadn't been regularly disposing of the emotional garbage and it had spilled over into their sex life.

The couple carried that same garbage from Suburbia, U.S.A., to Puerto Vallarta, Mexico, and they still really didn't want to touch each other. Touching means disturbing the garbage; it means at least admitting that it's there because you have to go past it or get rid of it to get where you want to be.

These solve-all trips seldom work. In fact, if a couple is at the stage where they want a fixit trip, they are probably at the stage where they need to do serious anger work. A romantic trip should occur *after* the partners have done their emotional work; it should be a celebration.

Detente

In another case, that of Gene and Denise, the distancing between them was becoming more pronounced. It hung politely poised between them like a cloud, grey and threatening one moment and briefly lightened the next as it drifted in the path of a fleeting sun ray.

The breach in their sexual intimacy wasn't being discussed and they continued to treat each other with consideration. But these actions gradually, almost imperceptibly, began to assume a mechanical quality.

They both confided later that feelings of anxiety and unreality permeated their relationship during this period. Tacitly, they established and settled-in on a routine in which one of them would go to bed earlier than the other — or, if they couldn't gracefully avoid preparing for bed at the same time, one would pointedly remark, "This has been a long day and I'm exhausted; the bed will really feel good tonight." Weeks of these "tonights" turned into months.

One night, as a fixit emergency measure, Gene suggested they have a few drinks, hoping this would help them to loosen up. It did — until Gene made the sexual approach. Denise "complied" but the sex was a failure that left them both more angry and even further apart.

For Gene, there was physical release but no emotional satisfaction because his own suppressed anger and his awareness of Denise's perfunctory response far outweighed the momentary sexual pleasure. For Denise, there was no orgasm, so physical frustration added to her anger at Gene's too-obvious pre-planning of the sex. Their bodies had come to the party but their hearts were elsewhere.

In cases of fixit copulation such as this, the partners can either pretend it was fine or be honest and admit it was a disaster. They pretended.

A Common Cycle

The cycle we see in motion here is a common one: Stored anger, physical distancing, sexual problems, more anger, repetition of the cycle.

After a few more abortive attempts at lovemaking, months apart, Gene and Denise sought marriage counseling. They had private and joint sessions with the therapist.

In a joint session, Denise said, "I can't just make love 'out of the blue.' After not being touched for months, I can't just turn on and off like a faucet." She added pensively, "Sometimes, I tried my darndest but it just wasn't any good — even when I did climax."

Gene retorted, "It wasn't anything great for me either." He looked at the counselor, asking, "Did you ever try to make love to a board?"

The anger dynamics in cases such as theirs is that one partner occasionally initiates sex. The spouse, who has also been waiting months to have sex, goes along with it. Neither enjoys it because they are really just using sex in an attempt to reverse the distancing between them and to get close again, plus relieving a physical tension.

If they dealt with the anger first, they wouldn't have to try to get back together; nothing could keep them apart.

Identifying the Anger

In a private session, Gene started to identify his anger. He admitted he was angry at Denise because she belittled the business venture he had launched the previous year — opening his own TV repair shop. He said she nagged about the long hours he spent at the shop and about its low financial yield. He also resented her unspoken messages that he was a "clod" as a lover. He added, "She holds herself back sexually."

Denise had no difficulty naming the major causes of her anger, although she had never aired them. She was angry because Gene "expects me to be a traditional female — the good wife, the always available sexual mate, the servant, and so on."

And Gene had been right, she did have a great deal of anger about his business and its income potential and, specifically, was angry that he had used money out of their household and recreation budget to help cover shop expenses. And she was angry about his "lack of finesse" in lovemaking which she described as "no foreplay whatsoever, just erection, insertion, ejaculation."

With guidance, both Gene and Denise were able to get to the roots of this and their other angers and to begin sorting things out. By re-creating and acting out the anger situations in private therapy sessions, both were able to identify when their angers had begun and when they had started holding them in.

Separately, each partner recognized that it was when they started to bury their angers that the physical distancing had begun.

In joint sessions, they now started expressing their upsetness about the real issues and completing the angers.

In the first of these encounters, they had difficulty making eye contact as they began to verbalize their resentments. Denise was more assertive in her expression than Gene, who fumbled with his words.

Denise initially was very rigid in her posture and spoke in a staccato manner as she recited her "I resent you for . . ." statements but, as she proceeded, became more relaxed, letting herself become emotionally involved in the anger. As she continued, Gene became obviously agitated and defensive, looking away from her and shifting around in his seat.

"You Don't Have To Change"

The therapist realized that Gene didn't want to hear Denise's litany of resentments because he was equating her expression of the angers as a decree that he would have to change. The therapist told him, "You're not the accused. You're not on trial — and you don't have to change because she is angry."

After asking Denise to repeat her last-stated resentment: "I resent your taking money from the household budget to cover shop expenses," the therapist asked Gene to immediately respond with, "I hear your resentment and that doesn't make me guilty, that doesn't make me bad, and it doesn't mean I have to change."

The counselor asked Denise to repeat her statement again, with an addition: "I resent your taking money from the household budget to cover shop expenses — and you don't have to change."

At first, Denise didn't want to complete the statement this way because her purpose was indeed to get Gene to change.

Voicing a resentment can be a manipulative act which carries the message: "From now on, you'd better shape up." When this is the purpose of voicing the anger, it isn't effective as anger work because it's not honest completion of the anger; it's blaming, or manipulation.

Even if the "accused" does change the resented action, the accuser will quickly replace that resentment with another because the underlying anger, the real issue, is still present.

The only valid reason for expressing anger is to get it out of the system.

When Denise did agree to add the ". . . and you don't have to change" to her statement, she found, to her surprise, that her anger now was being released — because the release was no longer dependent on external circumstances, on Gene's changing.

Gene, too, was hoping for change; he wanted Denise to change her opinion about her anger. He told her, "I resent your being angry about my using some of the money for the business. The shop is for us and for our future — how can you be angry? That's not reasonable or logical. I didn't use the money for a spree."

The therapist helped Gene realize that whether or not Denise's anger was justified or logical was not the point. The point was that her anger existed. He told Gene, "It's too late to think you can change her anger; she's already angry. Denise is merely expressing her feelings and you're trying to get her to change her opinion about her feelings. The two don't mix: opinions are cognitive, feelings are emotional."

The rest of the hour was spent in a training session. Denise practiced adding the ". . . and you don't have to change" phrase to her resentment statements. She also practiced responding to Gene's statements with, ". . . and I don't have to change my opinion about my anger."

Gene practiced the "that doesn't make me guilty, and I don't have to change" response and also practiced telling Denise, ". . . and you don't have to change your feelings about your anger."

These exercises can be taught and learned but, like most lessons, they require practice. It is not enough to merely hear or read them; it is the practice which allows them to become internalized and which produces the ever-increasing positive results. Eventually, these new attitudes and responses become automatic but it takes practice to arrive at that point.

The training session helped Gene and Denise realize that it is important not to get hooked into the other's anger. That hook, as part of a "game," can deter the other person's completion of the anger.

At their few remaining sessions, Gene and Denise progressed rapidly toward resolution of their problems. As they cleansed their systems of the angers, they were able to begin communicating again. They became willing, even eager, to make compromises about specific situations. They also decided — freely chose — to make some changes in certain actions.

There developed between them a happy spirit of collaboration, of "being in it together" as they consciously directed their energies to strengthening and building up the relationship rather than weakening and tearing it down. In this new atmosphere, it became natural and easy for Denise to express her sexual wants and needs to Gene, something she had not been able to do in the past.

With this confiding of her needs and wants, Gene saw that he *had* been a "clod" sexually. In the new atmosphere of openness and cooperation, he was more than willing to work at changing that situation and Denise no longer felt a need to "hold back."

All of this occurred in the span of only *six weeks*.
When they walked out of the last session, Denise spon-
taneously slipped her arm through Gene's. He hugged
it to his side with his own. The distance between them
had evaporated.

Fixit Sex Manuals

Some couples attempt to revive ailing sex by referring to sex manuals that promise people a more active
and enjoyable sex life.

There is nothing especially wrong with married couples following the suggestions in the manuals — except
that the results aren't lasting if there are underlying
problems in the relationship. It's like treating a skin
rash with an ointment rather than treating or elim-
inating the cause of the rash.

A variety of sexual techniques can be an embellish-
ment to an already healthy relationship that merely
needs perking up. But improved sexual techniques
don't improve sexual intimacy unless emotional intimacy is improved first or simultaneously.

If the fixit attempt begins and ends with the step-by-
step directions for having bigger and better orgasms,
then this measure is only a Band-Aid. Focusing on
technique becomes another way to avoid facing issues.
This approach may get a couple through a few sexual
encounters and allow them to "perform" with everything clicking along on cue, but it won't keep clicking.
Human beings are not machines.

"Physical" Sex Problems

Untended anger can lead to "physical" sex problems
in one or both partners. These problems include impotence — the inability to achieve or maintain erection, or

premature ejaculation in the male, and, in the woman, frigidity, in which she cannot be aroused or cannot achieve orgasm. There is great variance in the manifested symptoms, not only between individuals but within the same person at different times.

Premature Ejaculation

A construction worker, Merle, made an appointment for counseling because he was experiencing premature ejaculation. Merle was very much the macho type and also loved to brag.

As a teen-ager, Merle's father was prone to bragging to Merle — when Merle's mother was out of earshot — about his sexual accomplishments both before and during marriage. Merle followed this same pattern, including having occasional "one-night stands" with waitresses who worked in the local pub where he "hoisted a few with the boys" or with the office clerk in the construction office.

He told the therapist he didn't have the premature ejaculation problem in the extra-marital affairs: "I can go on as long as I want to with them," he said, "so I know everything's OK down there. The only reason I'm here is because the family doc said I should see a shrink about this. Seeing a shrink doesn't make sense to me . . . but I guess it won't hurt anything."

The example of Merle experiencing the premature ejaculation with his wife and not with the "one-night stands" is not an isolated one. Many persons who have sexual problems only experience those problems with the person they really care about. This demonstrates the power of the emotions.

Merle's somewhat defensive stance about his decision to "see a shrink" was not surprising. Macho types commonly have resistance to counseling or to admitting problems because that breaks down the false front machoism puts up. Machoism is a pretense of being strong. The macho person is generally fearful of closeness, and machoism itself promotes distancing.

After Merle's initial remarks, the session proceeded. Here is a condensed version:

Merle: I don't really need counseling. There wouldn't be any problem if she didn't put me off and make me wait so long in between. That's why I don't have as much control when we do get with it. (Accusingly, as if talking to his absent wife, he added,) I had the erection, she just couldn't come fast enough.

Therapist: How do you feel about her not wanting sex very often?

Merle: Well, I think she just grew up in a screwy family. She thinks sex is dirty. I don't think her father has gotten near her mother since he knocked her up when she got pregnant with my wife.

Therapist: It looks like you don't want to acknowledge any rejection on her part, that you would rather explain or excuse her behavior than look at how you feel toward her for being the way she is. Is it difficult for you to acknowledge your reactions toward her? What do you do with your feelings toward your wife?

Merle: Anytime I try to lay them on the table, I get talked out of it.

Therapist: When was the last time you tried to talk about them?

Merle: A few years ago she had an abortion. And she just went and made the arrangements without telling me about it. I didn't know anything about it until she called and asked me to pick her up, because she was too woozy to drive, after it was all over. I didn't say much then but later I wanted to talk about it. I brought it up once in awhile.

Therapist: What was her reaction when you tried to talk about it?

Merle: She put me down because I couldn't forget about it. She said, "That's in the past and I don't want to hear it." So I just shut up.

As the session continued, it also came out that Merle had then started spending more time with his buddies at taverns. He said, "I don't have to think about it when I'm drinking and shooting the breeze with the boys." Now letting his feelings come out, he went on, "But when I go to bed and try to have sex, I think about it again. I wonder whether she's going to get pregnant. That other time I thought she was on the pill. I don't want her getting pregnant and having another abortion.

"I tried to put those feelings away like she wanted me to but I couldn't."

At the second session, the therapist said, "I'd like to invite you — today — to not put away those feelings you talked about, but to bring them out instead."

Using the empty-chair technique, he asked Merle to express the feelings about his wife and the abortion directly to her. Merle had gotten some temporary relief at the first session by starting to explore his suppressed anger so he said he was "willing to give this my best shot."

He approached it as something that could build up his macho image of himself rather than detract from it. "OK," he told the therapist, "let's grab the bull by the horns."

For thirty minutes, he expressed his anger to his wife in the empty chair. He told her about the abortion itself and his further hurt that she hadn't consulted him. He also told her he resented her for making him feel "less than a man" because he couldn't forget about it — because he couldn't control his thoughts and feelings about it.

As he unloaded the angers, the relief clearly showed on his face, in his body, his voice. Although Merle's wife wasn't willing to discuss the situation or to come to counseling with him, that didn't prevent him from working through his own unfinished anger.

Merle himself made the connection between not being able to control his feelings about the abortion and not being able to control his sexual "staying power," as he called it. He said, "I guess I don't need to be a . . . what did you call it? . . . a premature ejaculator . . . anymore."

If the client doesn't make the connection, the therapist elicits it by asking, "What do you think has happened?" and then asking him or her to verbalize the breakthrough with a statement such as the one made by Merle.

For Merle, who had been willing to work hard at the exercises, it only took two exercise sessions to complete his anger.

The therapist then asked Merle to simply confide to his wife that night that he had taken care of his feelings about the old abortion issue and that she wouldn't have to worry about him bringing it up anymore.

Merle called in a few days to report to the therapist: "My wife seemed relieved when I told her I had put away the abortion thing once and for all. She even let me know later that she wanted to 'get it on.'

"We had our best time in bed in years. I don't know what was different — we did the same things — but it was better than a cold beer on a hot day. I was back to my old self and everything was right on target!"

Frigidity

In another case involving a Yuppie (Young Urban Professional) couple, it was the wife who was experiencing the "physical" problems. The husband initiated the move to seek marriage counseling but they both came to the first session.

The husband was a broker in his mid-thirties who was beginning to enjoy the financial fruits of his career as well as the fringe benefits in terms of professional respect, social contacts and increasingly interesting and challenging accounts.

When the husband had called to make the appointment, he had said, "My wife never achieves orgasm. She seems disinterested. She acts like sex is an obligatory service she provides for me. And she's usually very . . . dry . . . when we have intercourse."

In joint therapy, he softened the statements, saying, "We are having a problem lately in our sex life. It's not the same as it used to be. It seems like my wife isn't getting any enjoyment out of sex."

The wife needed no prodding to respond. She said, "All he's got to do is work at his 8 to 5 job and then he's free of work and responsibility for the day. He can get turned on in five seconds and he expects me to feel the same way.

"I'm tired of all my multiple roles: I work, too, and I have a demanding job as program director for a health agency. But most of the household tasks still fall to me. I'm the one who takes the baby to the day-care center and to doctor's appointments. I'm the hostess who arranges the dinner parties — and cooks — for my husband's business associates and their wives.

"Women's lib hasn't done a thing for me."

Her blaming and complaining provided no relief for her hurt, frustration and anger. She was whining about the situation, not emoting her anger. She wasn't letting herself have an emotional orgasm, so to speak, and this carried over into her sexual responses.

It took two sessions for her to move from complaining to expression of feelings in an assertive, productive way. She communicated her anger at the inequity of the marital workload distribution in a straightforward, non-blaming manner.

Being rid of her anger, she was then able to stop playing martyr; she hired a part-time maid, which they could well afford, and she asked her husband to commit himself to doing specific housekeeping and parenting tasks that would make the home workload more even.

She also told him she thought they should start "dating again" and spend at least some time doing pleasurable, romantic things together.

He was pleasantly surprised. This was the girl he had married — full of fire and spunk and excitement.

With some negotiation, and with her also making concessions to some of his angers about her not participating in activities that were important to him, they devised a mutually agreeable plan of action.

"Let's start with dinner tonight at that new eastside restaurant we saw advertised," he said.

Separate and Equal

In another case, the woman, unlike the wife above, had no admitted anger at her husband. She said, "He's the best husband in the world. I love him. I think he's wonderful. But I just don't like having sex anymore."

As the session proceeded, she did, very reluctantly, begin to identify anger areas and express them, but this was difficult for her. Each faint-voiced verbalization of anger carried a tag phrase such as, "but he is so kind and thoughtful in other ways" or "he's always supported me in everything I do . . . it makes me feel so disloyal . . . and so guilty."

This case brings up a point that cannot receive too much emphasis for it is one of the most important principles of this entire course. Love and anger are separate emotions and they are separate and equal.

Many of us have been conditioned in one way or another to believe that anger cancels out love, or that we shouldn't get angry at someone we love.

This is not true.

The two feelings exist simultaneously in most of us most of the time although each takes dominance at different times.

It is not realistic to expect ourselves or anyone else to possess only the "positive" emotions. If we assume this position, we pay the price in guilt when we experience very normal feelings of anger or other "down" emotions.

An exercise in resentment and appreciation designed to counteract this lopsided view was suggested for the woman above. The husband was asked to participate in the session, in which both were directed to make statements such as: "I appreciate you for remembering birthdays, anniversaries, special occasions and I resent you for not consulting me in major purchase decisions" or "I appreciate you for supporting my business decisions and for running a wonderful house and I resent you for treating my relatives as intruders."

The use of the conjunction "and" rather than "but" is important here. "But" would indeed tend to cancel out the appreciative phrases, while "and" shows that the feelings are separate and equal.

In therapy, the husband in this case initially said, "I don't have any anger." The therapist challenged him: "You don't? What do you do with it? You've been married 20 years — what have you done with your anger?

It's impossible to live with someone one week, much less 20 years, without having some anger."

Any couple whose marriage seemingly flows without a ripple, who never exchanges cross words, may not be as happy as they seem. Beneath the surface of the calm, still water may be a whirlpool of unexpressed anger.

The therapist's challenge to the husband helped start the couple's flow of expression. As they practiced the appreciation and resentment exercise, both were able to complete previously unvoiced resentments. They also voiced appreciations which they hadn't been accustomed to verbalizing.

Their problems were not deep seated; their relationship was basically very healthy. The resentments, once out in the air, evaporated. The wife said, "This is quite surprising. I really don't see why ventilating those really very petty little angers of mine would have an effect on my sexual feelings but . . . I just know that the 'sex problem' has been solved."

The therapist responded, "Express one emotion honestly and directly and you're able to express them all."

Impotence

A socially prominent woman from New York made an appointment with a psychologist while on vacation with her husband in the Southwest. Louise exhibited the kind of social ease and grace which comes from generations of proper breeding and landed money.

She told the counselor, "I'm really concerned about Allen's impotency problem. I do everything I can to help him. I've read all the books, tried all the techniques, and nothing seems to help."

Husband Allen, a large man physically, was a very successful attorney, brilliant in the courtroom but not very verbal about personal feelings. He gave the impression of being strong and imperturbable.

Louise let it be known in "casual" conversation that Allen was a few rungs below her on the social ladder.

In a private therapy session, Allen revealed his anger at Louise's habit of putting him in an inferior position. She made him feel inadequate with many double-edged remarks and with facial expressions, he said. "She likes to lord it over me in public and in private," he remarked.

In sessions alone with the therapist and together, the partners began to reveal the roots of their angers.

A summary of that scenario is that early in the marriage, Allen had had a brief extra-marital affair which had ended when it was discovered by Louise. She forgave him and the incident was never mentioned again.

But the emotional causes and effects of that infidelity were never dealt with, and this took its toll on the relationship. It was at this time that Louise had begun to use her lineage, her social register prominence to lord it over Allen. It was her way of getting even. He, in turn, eventually responded subconsciously by becoming impotent.

The dynamics operating here are that Allen felt anger toward Louise but instead of giving the anger to her, he transmuted it to guilt and retroflected it back upon himself. This occurred rather easily because he still felt guilt about the early affair. Part of him said she had a right to treat him the way she did and that because of the affair he had no right to get angry at her about anything ever. The other part of him was angry.

He then did to himself what he really wanted to do to Louise — cause her to be frustrated, in this instance, sexually. It was again an example of retroflection.

In retroflection, we do to ourselves what we'd really like to do to someone else. Wanting to hit the other person, we hit ourselves.

Allen was also retaliating. The hidden message he was transmitting to her was, "I don't care what your ancestry is, you aren't desirable to me — and I will not get an erection."

The case illustrates that the partner with the problem is actually the one who is in the position of power.

As a result of not processing his anger in a healthy way, Allen lost his potency or sexual power. And the impotence became another form of sexual power. In effect, he was saying to Louise, "I'm doing the best I can. I guess if you were really more loving, I wouldn't be having this problem."

She took on the responsibility of doing "everything I can to help him."

Impotence is often used as the weapon for a coup in ongoing marital warfare. The person may "triumph" in battle, but are there any "winners?"

The personalities and backgrounds of Allen and construction worker Merle were vastly different, but there is a striking similarity in their cases. Both were unwilling to accept the responsibility for their own sexual potency. They blamed their wives.

Spousal Guilt

The wife of an impotent husband may acccept this blame, responding with guilt feelings.

She may tell herself, "How can I be mad at the poor guy? I know he's frustrated. I'm frustrated too, but I shouldn't get angry at him." Or, a husband may buy into his frigid wife's nonverbal message that, "You've got to work harder at it, take care of me better — then maybe I can have an orgasm." He may spend inordinate amounts of time and energy trying to please her, to no avail.

The persons with the problems are in the positions of power in these situations.

It is this reluctance to take responsibility for one's own sexual power which causes some people to consult a medical doctor. It is easier to think of a problem as physical rather than emotional. That way, the problem can be handed to a doctor to fix it. (We are not referring to cases where there has been injury to the genital organs or a disease that affects sexuality, in which case recourse to clinical medical intervention is warranted.)

Working it Out

The problems existing between Louise and Allen were complicated. The angers had been repressed for a long time and the mechanisms each had called into play to suppress them were intricate.

It was during their fourth therapy session together that the breakthrough occurred.

Allen — strong, imperturbable — allowed himself to reveal his inner feelings to Louise: "I resent you for the emphasis you place on 'pedigrees,' on 'labels,' on 'who came to the party.' I am angry at your innuendos about my family . . ." He paused and swallowed, continuing haltingly, ". . . and I am hurt that you don't really seem to care about me or what I do . . ." Tears came from Allen's eyes, his voice was choked.

Louise had never seen this aspect of her husband, this very human, vulnerable side. The effect this had on her was rapid — and common.

When one partner's defense system begins to crack and break, the other's also quickly falls apart. What happens is that the game of offense and defense is interrupted with honest risk-taking action in which real feelings are exposed.

Louise also started crying as she responded, "I'm hurt, too. I never felt like you really loved me after the affair." Then, her voice revealed her acute awareness of Allen as a human being with feelings, as the man she married, rather than as an adversary. She said, "Oh, my dear, I do appreciate your career, your integrity in your law practice, your successes — and your honest failures. And I care about you."

Allen was very moved. "You've always helped me — and not only with 'connections'," he said, even managing a chuckle at the "connections" phrase. He added, "You've always inspired me."

Words, tears, laughter and touching flowed between them.

The therapist had stepped into the background when their free exchange had begun. When there was a relaxed lull, he asked them to complete the session for that day with an exercise of "appreciation only" statements.

For many people, it is as difficult to express appreciation as it is to express resentment, and the whole keyboard of emotions is necessary for balance and harmony.

Much progress had been made by Louise and Allen; the major breakthrough had been achieved. But there were still details to be dealt with before they could arrive at a clean and clear state. For one thing, there was the matter of Allen's early affair. That incident had never been worked through.

The new openness between them now made it possible to address this painful bit of unfinished business and successfully complete it by doing anger exercises on the still-stored feelings relating to the affair.

Extra-marital Affairs

When there is an infidelity in a couple's marital history, there is, almost without exception, unfinished stored anger — usually in both partners. This is one of the most common sources of subverted anger to surface in therapy.

The roots, causes, effects and manifestations of anger attendant on infidelity — before, during and after the actual act of unfaithfulness — are complex and usually convoluted. Drawing from hundreds of cases, we will mention just a few of the most common characteristics of the related angers.

First of all, the affair itself is usually an anger response, an acting out of resentment against the spouse by the unfaithful partner. This is commonly denied at first in therapy. The person who committed the infidelity is likely to say, defensively, "I didn't have any anger or resentment; I just wanted a 'change'."

The person is forced to delve deeper when the therapist challenges this, saying, "Oh, is that right? Then, why didn't you have the affair the year before, or the month before?"

In the majority of cases, a connection is found between the affair and something specific that was going on in the marriage at that time, something that was causing anger and hurt.

Another common characteristic of an anger-influenced affair is the tendency to let the affair be "discovered." An affair is one way of getting even with a spouse and the retaliation cannot be savored if the mate doesn't know about it.

This explains why unfaithful husbands or wives who aren't discovered often confess the incident themselves. In effect, they are saying to their spouses and to themselves: "I'm honest and open; I've made a confession; I'm clean and clear. Now, you have to deal with it."

That type of disclosure has one true intent: Hurt the other person. There are more productive ways for the erring partner to work out his/her anger and guilt.

With disclosure, one of the following usually occurs: (a) the other spouse uses the affair as an excuse for also having one; (b) the injured partner constantly refers to the affair, "throws it up" and uses it as the major weapon in a never-ending attempt to punish; (c) the spouse doesn't ever refer to the act again (as in the case of Louise and Allen) but uses it as inner fuel to provide punishment in other ways; or (d) the spouse "forgives," they "patch-up" the relationship and continue on.

The problem with "forgiveness" not accompanied by a true expression of feelings is that both parties still have feelings of blame, anger, guilt or hurt that need to be expressed and these cause later problems.

If an extra-marital affair has already been disclosed and the couple wishes to deal with it, it can serve as an impetus for positive anger work that can improve the relationship.

The intellectual memory of the incident does not disappear. But once the anger attached to it has been completed, it will no longer push the emotional buttons when it is recalled.

Another very frequent source of hidden anger seen in marriage counseling is premarital pregnancy. Anger related to a premarital pregnancy affects not only the man and woman at the time but affects the future tenor of the marriage. It is apt to involve the child born of that pregnancy and the other children born of the union as well (this will be discussed later when we consider the effects of anger on family relationships).

Risks and Growth

We are beginning to understand just how powerful the emotion of anger really is. This power can also propel growth and development in a relationship. This was true in the case of Bob and Pam, a couple in their late twenties. Their distancing had started shortly after the first of the year and, by mid-March, Bob decided it was time to put an end to it.

He awakened Pam in the middle of the night and said, "I want to talk. I'm tired of this 'no loving' situation." Pam responded with anger about Bob's waking her from a sound sleep. "This has been going on for more than two months and now you wake me up to talk about it. I feel the same way but it's waited this long and it can wait until tomorrow. I'm going back to sleep."

But, after getting out her anger about Bob's choice of timing, Pam felt a sense of exhilaration from the ventilation and was ready to talk. They were both ready to start dealing with issues.

It had all started at a party. Bob resented the fact that he felt Pam had "put me down" with a flippant remark "in front of my friends."

She was angry because he "flirted with Jason's cousin" at the same party. They vigorously exchanged these "I resent" remarks for some time and then, at a certain point, they looked at each other and collapsed, laughing, into each other's arms.

The source of their anger wasn't in itself deep-rooted or serious but their feeding of it for weeks in storage had been causing it to assume serious proportions.

The power — the positive force — of anger can be seen in the way they resolved the situation: it was Bob's anger that gave him the courage to start the confrontation and it was also their anger that allowed them to bring the rankling factors into focus, to crystallize and verbalize them.

In the book "Sexual Intimacy" (Seabury Press, New York) by Andrew M. Greeley, the author writes, "Conflict is an absolutely indispensable mechanism for growth in intimacy. It is the way two lovers disclose to one another the 'imperfect fit' in their physical and psychological needs. It is a means for disclosing to each other aspects of their personalities that have previously been hidden.

"It not merely releases the inevitable tensions that build up in a shared life. It is also a manifestation of love, for conflict between lovers is a means by which they say to one another, in effect, that their love and trust is so great that they are not afraid to reveal to each other their anger and they have no need to hide the raw edges of their personalities."

It wouldn't require the impetus of anger for us to reveal ourselves to each other if we were perfect creatures who kept our emotional systems clean hour-by-hour, day-by-day. But even the healthiest of human beings haven't yet evolved to that degree.

For those who aim to move closer to the ideal, the rewards are tremendous. Anger can be a valuable catalyst but it demands risk-taking. When Bob woke Pam up in the middle of the night, he took the risk of making the situation much worse. But, rather than taking a sleeping pill or trying to get some troubled sleep, he took that risk.

When we take the risk, we are saying to the other person, "I honor you by taking a risk. I respect you by taking a risk. I trust you by taking a risk. I respect our relationship by taking a risk."

A relationship that is not safe enough to be at risk is not a healthy relationship. Healthy relationships can stand risk; they thrive on them. Taking risks with our loved one keeps proving we love each other. If we don't take the risks, we will have, at best, a very bland relationship. How can the other person really know how we feel unless we take the risk of expressing?

Despite the truth of the above, risk-taking is fearful business. It is really saying to the other, "I am giving you me naked. Shoot away if you want to, but I'm going to trust that if you do, I can survive it."

When the sincere risk is taken, there is an electricity in the air between the partners, a "crackling" in the room that gives the clear message: "This is important."

We believe there is no one who is not attracted to this kind of trusting-in-the-face-of-risk in a very positive way. When we are willing to trust enough to risk, we are almost never shot down. It is only when we are manipulating or in a power play that the other person responds in like manner.

When the risk is taken in this way, it clears the system and the air. An established relationship can feel like new. Yet it is better than a new relationship precisely because it is not new. Much of the major "testing" of each other has already been done and these risk-taking forays simply serve to deepen and broaden the union.

EXERCISES

Exercise 1. Angry Sex.

Review your sexual activity with your partner. Does sex often occur right after an angry fight? Do you often "give up" (put away) your anger to participate in sex? Do you often feel frustrated after sex?

During sex, notice whether you feel passive or detached or resentful, angry or hostile. Are you or your partner often much more aggressive (angry) after being sexually repelled?

Exercise 2. Identifying Fixit Measures.

Make a list of fixit methods you or your partner have used as "emergency measures" to try to patch up your relationship. What were the results? Notice the frequency of "favorite" fixit devices which you both use and the conditions under which each measure is used.

Exercise 3. Taking the Hooks Out of Anger.

Think about your anger toward a significant other person in your life. Make what you are angry about very specific in your mind (e.g., "I am angry that you didn't pay attention to me when I was sick").

Now, see if you are willing to own up to your anger without the demand that the other person change his/her behavior. Try some sentences such as, "I am angry at you for . . . and you don't have to do anything about it."

Notice any hesitancy or resistance to giving the other person permission to remain as he or she is. If there is resistance, chances are that you prefer to manipulate the other person rather than complete your own anger.

Exercise 4. Not Getting Hooked by Another's Anger.

Remember the last time you were on the receiving end of someone's anger. Note whether you felt guilty for their anger or defensive about receiving it. If you felt either, you have been hooked into their anger and are under its control.

To unhook yourself, mentally and verbally rehearse some responses to the other person's anger: "I hear your anger and understand what you are angry about" or "I can handle your being angry at me right now" or "I hear your anger and will allow you to have it — without my feeling guilty."

Exercise 5. The Needs Survey.

Make a "needs" list and have your partner make one that involves the whole area of intimacy and affection. This will include but by no means be limited to sexual desires. After each list has been privately developed, sit together and share and discuss the lists.

Select an exercise from any of those on the previous pages and once a day for one week practice it. At the end of the week, discuss the results of such practice.

7

ANGER AT HOME, WORK AND PLAY

In previous chapters, we have focused mainly on the angers spawned of our most intimate personal relationships because it is these which affect us so intensely.

But unfinished resentments and angry hurts can also have a very unpleasant and sometimes debilitating effect on our other family relationships, our business life and our social life.

These unresolved angers may be rooted in our one-to-one relationships and carried over to damage these other areas, or they may be directly conceived within one of these other areas of our lives. We will explore a few of these situations.

Pre-Marriage Pregnancy

Earlier, we referred to a common source of anger — pre-marriage pregnancy — which can powerfully affect not only the couple involved and their marriage but the child of the pregnancy and later children as well. Let's look at the anger dynamics.

The first seeds of anger poison are planted in the woman when she learns she is pregnant and, in the man, when it is revealed to him. The woman may feel,

"How could he do this to me? He got me pregnant and I'm the one who is physically imprisoned; the baby is in my body."

When the man is told, he may respond with angry feelings of: "Why did she let this happen? Why did she let us have sex when it wasn't 'safe'?" He may even retreat from the relationship at first — which is hurtful to the woman, who says or feels, "I thought he loved me; I thought we were going to get married anyway."

Both are blaming the other to one degree or another and, usually, the anger is not addressed. Instead, they may decide to go ahead and get married. Most couples who make this decision then proceed to convince themselves that they actually were going to get married anyway. But they start off not knowing if they are really committed to the marriage.

Generally, there is a great deal of anger transmuted to guilt which influences the decision to marry. With the man it may take the form of: "I feel guilty, therefore I will marry her," and with the woman: "I feel guilty so I will get married for the sake of the child."

The major resentment factor for both relates to loss of free choice. They did have the choice about having sex, but they didn't make a conscious choice about the pregnancy. To both, it seems they were put in the situation and this can leave the man feeling manipulated and the woman feeling trapped.

There are also the couple's parents to deal with, and often more angers as a result of those encounters. And there are societal pressures with which to contend. No matter how permissive the social mores are, that tolerance doesn't seem to solve the situation emotionally.

The woman frequently resents the fact that the hurry-up wedding is very different from her fantasies of falling in love and getting married, and both resent starting married life already "tied down."

One or both of the partners may have hidden anger because they know, at least at a subconscious level, that they are not ready for the marriage emotionally or financially.

Under the best of circumstances, neither party emerges without resentments. But they put them aside and turn their attention to hasty wedding plans.

At this point, if they were able to focus on the angers and complete them it would be infinitely more productive than focusing on the marriage ceremony. If both openly expressed their angers toward each other in the manner we have described relating to other angers, their systems would then be clear and they could make a better decision about whether to marry or to make other arrangements that would best benefit them and the baby in the long run.

If they did this, the odds are they would opt for marriage. A couple with enough courage to face this high-risk situation of honest expression would probably admire and respect each other tremendously and want to marry if the relationship had something going for it in the first place.

This would be a very healthy basis on which to begin a lifetime relationship and their marriage would be starting on a firmer foundation than most.

However, this is seldom done. The incomplete angers are left to gnaw away at the marriage.

These angers last. In Anger Therapy, many couples have identified a pre-marriage pregnancy as the source and starting point of anger that is threatening the marriage 15, 25, even 35 years later.

These buried angers are a constant source of irritation, always ready to cause internal inflammation at the slightest reminder of the situation. Even the mere presence of the child born of that pregnancy can be an irritant because the child is a reminder that there is unfinished business between the parents. When the marriage hits a high-stress period, as marriages are prone to do intermittently, these stuffed angers flare up.

The child of the pregnancy is also going to be affected. First of all, this premaritally-conceived child will have a different place in the family than later children, a special place. This may be extremely subtle and the special place may be "positive" but it is always different.

Some parents may over-compensate by giving the child more attention, more love, more leeway than the other children. Or, one parent may over-protect the child — from the wrath of the parent whose anger stays close to the surface.

Perhaps the special place is negative. A father may be more quick to discipline this child. The mother may respond with an outburst such as, "You're always picking on Johnny. You never wanted him anyway." She may become over-protective of this special birth or she may be overly protective of her husband: "Don't make so much noise, Johnny, your father had a hard day." Or she may become extra-protective of her own position in the marriage.

All this "business" going on between the husband and wife makes it harder for them to do straightforward, uncluttered interacting with the child.

The child receives subtle messages which he or she can't interpret but which cause anxiety. The hidden message may be, "You shouldn't be here," or "You're an embarrassment to me with my friends."

These children grow up with a subconscious understanding that something is not right, that something (judgment, guilt, etc.) is being placed on them that doesn't belong to them. Being young, inexperienced and with no awareness of the complex situation in which they find themselves, they will, again subconsciously, attribute their uneasy feelings to something else, such as: "Everybody feels this way"; "It's my imagination" or "Parents are this way." The child may never know what has really been happening through the years.

The other children also sense the special place assigned to the first child and may comment on this among themselves: "Why does Mary always get to do such and such?"; or, "Dad's always got it in for Johnny." Sensing the difference between themselves and the other child may cause them to feel apprehensive.

When the parents make the original decision about how they are going to handle their anger about the premarriage pregnancy — when they decide whether they are going to openly deal with the anger or whether they are going to ignore it and store it — they are also making a decision about the way the family will live.

Right then, they are deciding whether or not they trust and respect each other enough to be honest and open. If they choose the subversive approach, the trust levels are damaged between them and their ensuing actions damage the trust levels of the children, especially the first-born.

Sooner or later — even on the deathbed — one of the parents usually divulges the truth to the child in question. Mother or Dad feels a need to "confess."

Children born of a pre-marriage pregnancy who later seek counseling often say, "I don't know why such a big secret was made of it" or "I was born 'early' and I always felt it affected the way my parents treated me."

If the parents had completed the emotions attendant on the situation in the beginning, they would not have continued to think of it as an incident and it would not have had an adverse influence on their family life.

Family "On His Back"

In a totally different family-life situation involving
hidden anger, the father of four, a successful architect,
sought counseling because he was in severe depression.

He was in a high-pressure job; his firm was constantly in tough competition with other firms to submit the
plans and bids that would land the most lucrative, most
prestigious contracts.

This man and his family had a sophisticated lifestyle.
They weren't wealthy but enjoyed all the privileges of
affluence: the home in the exclusive suburb, the four-
bedroom mountain getaway "cabin," four cars, boats,
extensive ski and scuba diving paraphernalia, frequent
travel, clothes and a country club membership.

But Dad was depressed, he was weary. As the affluence went up, the family consumption went up, always
staying a notch ahead of the income. Dad's energy level
was so low he was finding it more and more difficult to
go to work in the morning, to say nothing of garnering
the energy, the astuteness and the concentration necessary to go after new bids or even to direct the completion of current projects.

He felt caught and trapped in the spin of the affluence
and consumption spiral.

But instead of admitting his resentments toward his
family, he became depressed.

Below the conscious level, he was feeling, "They
think I've got a money tree somewhere," and, "This
will be coming at me forever." He had set himself up to
be the provider and to be able to provide no matter
what. The more they consumed, the more he provided
— and the more depressed he became.

At three consecutive therapy sessions, he kept denying any anger or resentment. He would speak only of
"pressure" and "depression." Finally, the therapist

asked if he would be willing to participate in a family exercise. Apathetically, he agreed.

When the family was gathered — the husband, wife, two high-school children and two younger children — the therapist asked Dad to lie down on the carpet face down. He told him: "I'm going to have your family members sit on you, pile on top of you. When the pressure is the same as what you feel emotionally, let me know."

One-by-one, they got on, and Dad showed no reaction. The therapist asked, "How does that feel?" Dad replied in a lifeless, emotionless voice, "Okaaaaay." It was a sigh. When the youngest daughter added her 95 pounds to the mountain of bodies, the counselor repeated the question. Dad answered in the same monotone: "Not too bad. This is just the way it feels all the time." The family stayed in the position for 30 more minutes and Dad still didn't react.

The exercise did have an effect on some of the other family members. Two of the children said it made them realize they'd been "sitting on Dad." But Dad still denied the anger. He said, "No, I don't feel any resentment; I just worry a lot. I just don't see how we're going to do it (keep the 'provisions' coming). I just want them to understand."

Even having the family physically "on his back" didn't get him in touch with his anger.

The following week, however, the man was totally changed; the effects of the exercises are sometimes not felt immediately. He said, "I'll never forget them all sitting on my back. That made the biggest impression on me of anything in my whole life. Why would I allow that?"

In following sessions, Dad expressed his resentments to each of the family members. All of them participated in the therapy and, at the last session, they all gathered together for a final all-family exercise.

The therapist directed the other members to give Dad a "body lift." They physically lifted him and held him just above head level. A body lift is a powerful way of showing support and this was a very healing exercise for Dad. When they lowered him gently to his feet, there was much hugging and some happy tears.

This man's case illustrates an important point. He was having trouble generating or maintaining energy for his job but the root of the problem was at home. It frequently is.

The Weak Partner

In another case, that of a husband and wife who were in business together, it was the wife who held on to her anger and she was the weak partner in their sales company. Again, it was a case of low energy and apathy.

In a sales business, a no-energy, no-enthusiasm approach can scuttle the company. The woman was using all her energy to keep her anger about her personal relationship with her husband under wraps.

In a private session with the therapist, she said, "I just don't have the drive I used to and my husband is making all the decisions and all the sales." Later in the session, she admitted, "My husband and I aren't getting along."

The therapist asked her to work on the personal situation first. Even though many of the irritating interactions between the woman and her husband occurred at work, the source of the anger was at home, that is, it was in their personal relationship.

The woman began to sort out and express her resentments through anger exercises both in therapy and on her own. The therapist worked with her to help her start to speak up and stand up for herself in matters of contention not connected to the business.

This taking charge of her own inner-power sources almost instantly translated itself into higher sales for her and also transmitted energy on down through the organization.

The woman's assumption of her co-leadership role — which was what the couple had planned when they formed the company — also served to perk up the husband. Both were able to function much better.

When the woman stopped being the weak partner in the relationship, she got out of the same position in the business. This also dissipated the source of a major resentment held by the husband because he wanted her to assume her share of responsibility and to take initiative in their joint venture. Their "getting along" problem was solved.

Primary Personal Relationships

Anger problems at work are frequently a substitute for unresolved anger in our primary personal relationships. These are the relationships with the people most important in our lives:

1. Parents — biological, step or adopted parents, grandparents, or others who take the place of parents.
2. Intimate significant others — mates, ex-mates, lovers, ex-lovers.
3. Children — biological, step or adopted.
4. Siblings.
5. Very close friends.

We are not saying job-related anger does not exist. It definitely does. But if we take care of our primary relationships, especially in the first two categories, we are not nearly as prone to get into bad situations with other people, including at work. Or, we are more able to handle the circumstances in a productive way.

Job Anger

One woman, Artie, who had done her anger work on her resentments at her ex-husband and was complete with that old business, found herself developing a great deal of anger at her boss.

Over a three-year period, she had been given and willingly accepted a steadily increasing workload and more and more responsibility in the business. But there had been no promotion or increase in pay. Resentments were starting to dig deep; there was hurt, anger and a feeling of betrayal.

There was also some guilt at the anger because of her other feelings about her boss — her awareness and appreciation of his professional ability and integrity and his personal consideration of her and other employees.

But she remembered what she had learned in Anger Therapy: both the anger feelings and the appreciation feelings were valid feelings, one did not cancel out the other. They were separate and equal.

Artie was the type who was assertive when it came to taking initiative in work planning and performance but passive about seeking compensation. But when the workload increased again, the inequity of the situation rankled deeply. After putting up with this rankling feeling for a few more months, she spoke to her boss about a promotion.

He responded with praise for her work — and a title-only promotion. "The economic situation," he explained. "But if there's a national upswing, then perhaps next year or the year after, there will be money for a slight increase."

The matter was apparently closed in her boss's mind. But not in Artie's. She broke her lifelong pattern of passiveness in this regard and did not let it drop. To keep the pay-raise issue open, she kept reminding her boss of his vague promise to at least consult with the financial department about the possibility of a pay increase. Her manner of doing this was not demanding, not hostile, just steady. Her boss finally did pursue the raise, a minimal one.

Artie still did not let the matter drop. She had taken the big step and she wasn't going to stop in mid-air. She said to her boss, "Even if it's not possible, we could at least ask for the higher raise. If we don't ask, there is no possibility of getting it." He put in the request.

Artie called her therapist (whom she hadn't been in touch with since she had completed her personal anger work earlier that year) and told him about it. "I feel so good. I wouldn't have respected myself if I hadn't done this and carried it through. Now, it's in the hands of the financial department and whatever happens I feel much better. I've done everything I can and now it's out of our office. I stood up for myself, and I didn't have to get in a huff about it."

Ten days later she called to say she had gotten the raise, a good one. The therapist said, "That's what I would call a $6,000 exercise." Discussing what had occurred, the therapist told her, "If you hadn't previously dealt with your old personal anger at your 'ex,' you might have used this situation as an excuse to put another notch of hate in your belt, displacing the old anger at your husband onto the boss and approaching him with a belligerent, self-defeating attitude.

"Or, you might have spent years getting even. Since you were in the clear with personal anger, you were able to deal with this in a positive way."

"Getting Even"

One man, a civil servant, did employ the "getting even" tactic; he "got even" by doing the poorest job possible. His performance and negative attitude resulted in his receiving the lowest ratings in his division year after year for many years.

The division director tried to fire him, but he sued, won and stayed on the job. He wouldn't work, he wouldn't leave.

Years before, as a young employee, he had been up for a promotion. When he didn't get it, he started "getting even" — and getting ulcers. When this government office adopted an official employee assistance and intervention program in which employees with work performance problems were given a mandate to "shape up or ship out," his supervisor documented his job performance and he had no choice but to talk to the program counselor.

The counselor referred him to an anger therapist. The anger was traced to the promotion incident and then traced back even further to anger at home. Because his primary relationship was full of unfinished business, he transferred his anger to the promotion bypass when that occurred. This gave him a "legitimate" place to which he could direct his anger.

Hidden Distraction

In another case, a secretary was consistently running behind schedule on her job. The woman had a poor work record. Most of her jobs had lasted less than a year. While she was doing lackadaisical daydreaming about "Why don't I feel better . . . I've been exercising . . .," the office work was piling up. By 10 a.m. on any given day, she was already "out of steam."

Her supervisor wanted to help her and convinced her to seek counseling. Her anger was identified as relating to one of the primary relationships, her unfinished anger at her mother.

She uncluttered her mind by completing the anger and was then able to focus on the job, approaching it with a new productive attitude that paid off in both career advancement and self-esteem.

Old angers are a distraction. Rather than being able to look at life with clarity, there is a multi-focus which blurs and distracts.

This secretary is no different from an attorney whose unresolved anger at home translates into an inability to take care of details in the office or to prepare briefs properly.

One man who had very effectively cleansed his system of old personal angers, was enraged about a real estate deal in which there had been verbal misrepresentation. He knew that, legally, he had no recourse. He also had no desire to put his system back into an anger-clogged state, so he used an anger exercise he had learned to unclog his system.

While driving through the city on a summer day, with the air conditioner on, the windows closed and the radio blaring, he started yelling his resentments at the steering wheel — where he had "placed" the person who was the object of his rage: "I resent you for lying to me, you (expletives deleted) . . ." Fifteen minutes of this finished the anger. He then left it at the car wash.

On a job, there are obviously certain givens which determine just how much we can do with our anger. We can't, for instance, just go around telling bosses how angry we are at them. But, if our primary personal relationships are in good order, we can defuse the volatile part of our work anger in private at home in a "safe" situation through the exercises. Then, we can approach bosses and supervisors in a non-manipulative, non-threatening, rational way that is much more likely to net positive results.

Once we have cleared the system, we may also see that, having done all we can about the work situation, it is time to look for another job or make a career change. If this is indicated, we can do this, too, in a more tranquil way than if weighted down emotionally with untended anger.

Anger at Play

Our social life can also suffer from the unfinished business at home. Consider the case of the husband who is always the life of the party. His consistent "cutting up" is a constant source of embarrassment to his wife. Both have resentments they deal with in subversive ways.

His endless "funny imitations" and other "center-stage" ploys at parties are a way to dominate her because he knows they upset her. Her embarrassment is her way to avoid dealing with her angers. They will continue this game until they uncover the motivations behind his being a clown and her being an embarrassed martyr who only continues to attend the parties because she feels it is a social obligation.

Other people reveal their anger in social situations by being sarcastic or acting superior. A social gathering is a perfect place to allow the put-down of your partner to "slip through the cracks" of a "humorous" remark, but the "punch" line is seldom misunderstood.

Being withdrawn can be another way of not dealing with anger. Remember the people you've seen sulking at the end of the couch?

Another example is the chronic complainer who is chewing on bitterness and spewing the venom from one end of the party to the other. He/she complains incessantly about: American manufacturers, the court system, the lack of good service at restaurants, the state of society and everything else.

The chronic late-arriver for engagements is also apt to be an angry person. A consistent pattern of tardiness is a passive-aggressive act, a manipulative power-play because the other person can't do anything about it. ("If I'm late, you just have to sit there and wait.") Forgetfulness (when there is no senility involved) is a similar manifestation of subverted anger ("Don't get so upset; I just forgot the Browns were expected," "I just forgot it was your birthday.").

There are countless other examples of anger-related social malfunctioning such as these, and they all produce poor results. They do nothing to resolve the angers — and nothing to add to the popularity of the perpetrators.

EXERCISES

Exercise 1. What Is Your Anger Response Today?

Write out the answers to the following question:
How do I handle my anger when it is related to my:
  Spouse or partner?
  Parent?
  Child?
  Sister or brother?
  Other relatives?

Exercise 2. Separating Business and Personal Angers.

A. Make a list of what bothers you at work.
B. Compare these irritations to similar reactions at home.
C. Note which ones you bring home to unload on spouse, kids.
D. Now make a list of what bothers you at home and analyze how many of these personal angers are being carried to work.

Exercise 3. Separate and Equal Exercise.

Four times a day, before meals and at bedtime, say to yourself, "Love and anger are separate and equal emotions."

8

ANGER AND ABUSE

In previous sections, we have seen some of the negative effects of unfinished anger on our systems and psyches. This examination of the harmful effects of simmering furies and ever-present aggravations on our emotional and mental health, on our appearance and on our personal and sexual relationships clearly indicates that storing anger results in abuse of self; it diminshes our potential to live fulfilling, productive lives.

Anger usually also plays a dominant role in substance abuse, is a strong catalyst in physical and sexual abuse, and is a frequent motivator in suicide. Suicide is the ultimate self abuse and, along with homicide, the ultimate angry act.

The casualty list of victims in these abuses is beyond measure. Not only do the angry persons inflict abuse on themselves but, to one degree or another, on everyone who happens to be in the fall-out zone of their particular form of abuse.

The various abuses we will discuss are complicated phenomena with a complexity of pscyho-social factors that influence their causes and their treatments.

We do not suggest that anger is the sole source of their development, nor that learning to express anger in a healthy manner will provide the sole or instantaneous answer or cure. The process by which these deeper abuses were conceived and reached maturation was not simplistic nor isolated from other events and factors in the individual's life. Neither is the recovery process.

What we do suggest, however — based on clinical experience with abusers and victims of abuse — is that there is an anger component which is a contributing factor in all of these conditions and that dealing with the anger factor can help break the cycle of abuse for both the abused and abuser.

Substance Abuse

Decades of research and empirical studies on alcoholism and addictions clearly show that there is a genetic predisposition to chemical dependency and that this disease has physical, psychological, mental, sociological and spiritual components.

It has also been demonstrated that when substance abuse has progressed to alcoholism or addiction, the free choice element has been eliminated and a total ongoing program designed specifically for the alcoholic or addict is usually needed to begin and maintain recovery.

Fortunately, there are many programs available such as Alcoholics Anonymous (with nearly 2 million members worldwide), Narcotics Anonymous, Cocaine Anonymous (all with corresponding programs for family members: Al-Anon, Alateen, Adult Children of Alcoholics, Nar-Anon, etc.) and other self-help programs. There are also an ever-increasing number of excellent public and private institutions dedicated to the alleviation of these diseases and to the alleviation of the effects of the disease both on the chemically dependent person and on co-dependents (partners or family members who get hooked into the alcoholic-addict's behavior).

The results of the continuing research on all aspects of chemical dependency have begun to revolutionize the whole area of the psychology of human behavior and emotions, both in understanding causes of deviations from the norm and treatments for a great variety of conditions.

Since this subject is so vast and since hundreds of fine books have been and are continuing to be written on this subject, we will not present case histories here. We have selected several books to include in our list of Related Readings (see pages 171-173).

Research and clinical practice have demonstrated, however, that anger and its suppression is always involved when abuse of any kind is present. When an alcoholic or addict begins a life of abstinence and commits himself or herself to a program of recovery, the anger exercises used throughout the book can be very beneficial to the recovery process. Family members — who have as much or more anger than the alcoholic/addict — can also benefit tremendously from the Anger Therapy techniques. The exercises are a powerful aid to healing the relationships that have been badly damaged and to opening up the lines of communication in relationships.

Physical and Sexual Abuse

It has only been in recent years that the widespread problems of physical and sexual abuse have begun to be addressed by scientific studies, self-help groups and by social and government agencies.

Battered wives, for example, have only recently received public encouragement to come out of their closets of pain to seek help. The same is true of the sexually abused.

Some researchers believe that sexual abuse of children is more widespread than physical abuse of them, which is currently estimated to affect more than 200,000 youngsters a year in the United States.

One researcher estimates that as many as 500,000 girls under age 14 are victims of sexual offenses each year.

Physical abuse cases are found at every level of society from the lowest to the highest, although the situation is often harder to detect in affluent families because victims have the means to seek private medical treatment.

Similarly, cases of incest and all other forms of sexual abuse are to be found at every socio-economic level and among people with every degree of skill, expertise and education.

Unfortunately, many sexual abuse victims are children who cannot themselves seek help. Media focus on the widespread incidence of sexual abuse of children is beginning to alert "outsiders" to the problem and to encourage them to report suspected cases to the proper authorities.

This is an important beginning but it is just a first step in combatting an enormous problem that will take the concerted effort of many agencies and individuals.

The depth and ramifications of these abuses is far too wide to allow us to do more than briefly touch on them here. But Anger Therapy exercises, if utilized, can ameliorate some of the lingering pain in abuse victims and can help the abuser to stop abusing.

The cases that follow are drawn from literally hundreds encountered in private and group therapy. In all of them, whether abused or abuser, anger was a key factor. Since an abuser is less likely to voluntarily seek counseling or therapy, we have seen abusers more frequently in institutional settings where they were receiving treatment or were incarcerated. We have seen the abuse victims in private practice or in group sessions arranged by agencies devoted to problems of abuse.

One fact clearly established by surveys and research and corroborated in clinical practice is that the great majority of physical and sexual abusers were either abused themselves as children or grew up in a household where they witnessed abuse. Those children who were abused in childhood who don't themselves become abusers often carry their victim role into adult life and pick spouses who will abuse them.

The Victim Role

One woman named Betty, who had become enmeshed in the victim syndrome, had been intermittently beaten by her father in childhood. Betty's mother had been the main whipping post during the father's drunken attacks, but Betty also received a share of the face-slapping, "knocking around" and severe "spankings" which sometimes left her sore and bruised for weeks. By the time she sought counseling, she was married to her second wife-beater.

In the course of therapy, Betty gained several insights, including awareness of the fact that her low self-esteem had its roots in her early abuse. She remembered feeling, "I must not be any good or my father wouldn't treat me like this" and "I really must be worthless because my mother isn't protecting me" and "I must not be very smart or I would know what to do."

She also was able to make the connection between her low self esteem and her need to marry men who would support that continuing belief.

In dealing with her anger and hurt, the therapist first helped her to accept the fact that, as a child, she had done exactly what she had had to do for survival. Her submission to the beatings didn't mean she was dumb or inadequate in dealing with the situation. Rather, it was the most adequate, the "smartest" response available to her at that time.

Lingering low self concepts entwined with feelings of guilty inadequacy are common in these cases. Youngsters involved in abuse situations take care of themselves the very best they can at the time — crawl under the bed, hide, say "yes," say "I'm sorry," be ingratiating, or to do whatever is necessary to get through the ordeal.

By working the exercise called "My response was the right one at the time" (see page 131), Betty was able to accept and internalize the truth that, as a child, she had responded in the only possible way.

Although the childhood response was the appropriate one at the time, there was a cost attached to having to deal with the abuse through passive, indirect methods.

In Betty's case, she was paying that price by marrying wife-batterers and continuing to be an abuse victim. Because she had never dealt with the repressed anger from the childhood abuse, she kept re-enacting it. (Other abuse victims respond by becoming abusers themselves. This is how the abuse cycle passes from generation to generation.)

In ensuing therapy sessions, Betty was able to express and complete her anger at her father *in absentia* through the same types of exercises we have discussed in previous chapters. Using "I" language, she told him very specifically what her feelings were and named the incidents connected to the feelings.

She also processed the anger at her mother for not protecting her. Then she worked out the anger at her physically abusive first husband and at her current spouse.

This was not easy; it had become a lifelong pattern for her to believe, "I must be terrible; otherwise, I would not keep getting my eyes blackened and my lip split and my teeth knocked out."

Abuse victims are true retroflectors; they let the anger they feel come back on themselves: "See, I deserve this. Yes, go ahead and beat on me. That proves that I'm not a worthwhile person."

Rather than get angry and take a stand, they will take the abuse. In some cases, they invite it and give it permission to occur. Meanwhile, they may be protesting verbally, but in a whining, complaining way which doesn't serve to finish the anger.

The next step in therapy was for Betty to face and deal with the fact that although her response as a child — when she was dealing with someone who was bigger, stronger, older and who had authority over her life — was the appropriate one then, it was not the appropriate response now.

The decision to change her response pattern meant that, among other things, Betty would have to give up being the "clean" party in the relationship. She would have to give up the role of self-righteous victim who could continue to heap guilt on the husband. When she became aware of her martyr role, she made the decision to seek a new response to abuse.

In fact, at this point, she became so eager to put her new self-confidence into action that she was prepared to dash home and "tell that S.O.B. where to get off." The therapist pointed out that, here, discretion was most definitely the better part of valor.

In these volatile situations, there is a need to obtain physical protection before confronting a physical abuser who has already demonstrated the very real danger he or she poses. This protection may range from contacting the sheriff's office or the police department to seeking help through an agency specializing in these cases, or to locating a shelter for battered wives.

We cannot emphasize this too strongly: *If you are currently a victim of abuse, seek help; don't attempt to handle it alone.* There are many professional organizations and agencies which offer such specialized help. They can be located in your city by contacting a central government health organization for information, a local "hotline" or "help-on-call" number, a crisis center or a law enforcement agency.

When the decision is made to stop being a victim, the abused can either leave the abusive environment or seek professional protection and assistance in attempting to convince the abuser to seek help.

Betty did contact an agency but was reluctant at first to follow the suggestion that she temporarily seek shelter in a home for battered wives and that she obtain a restraining order from the court stipulating that if her husband even approached her he would be subject to arrest.

After another beating, severe enough to hospitalize her for five days, she followed the agency suggestion. She sent her husband a letter telling him that help was available for him and enclosed a brochure from a helping agency and the name of a counselor he could contact.

The husband left the city. This is not uncommon because abusers live with so much guilt and self-loathing that, when their behavior begins to become known outside the home, especially to an agency that has any hint of "officialdom" attached to it, their bravado quickly fades.

Eventually, Betty obtained a divorce and, little by little, put her life back together. It took real willingness on her part and a commitment to the therapy.

Experience with thousands of cases of all varieties has demonstrated that the three categories in which the negative effects of anger are most difficult to overcome are those involving physical or sexual abuse and those involving the suicide of a loved one. Recovery requires concentrated work in therapy and continued practice of the new responses in daily living until these new responses become second nature.

Support groups for "Women Who Love Too Much," based on the book of that name by Robin Norwood, are springing up across the country as are treatment programs for women and men who have a pattern of "relationship addiction" — addiction to dysfunctional partners and to sick relationships in which their continuing hurt and their continuing loss of self esteem are guaranteed.

In a few years, after learning to live with herself and to like herself, Betty married again, this time to a healthy, non-abusive man.

Buried Battering Anger

Another woman, who had been a battered wife, sought counseling because she realized that her old anger at her ex-husband — which she thought had been "put to sleep" years before — was still close to the surface.

She told the therapist, "I was married for 15 years and have been divorced almost 15 years. I thought all the anger was gone."

After the divorce, she had gotten professional help in dealing with the shattered marriage and had undergone many positive attitudinal changes. She was now living a productive, happy life, free of major internal conflict and able to handle normal day-to-day frustrations extremely well.

During the post-divorce years, she and her ex-husband had gradually come to terms with each other and had even made mutual amends. The amends episode involved her journeying to visit her husband specifically for that purpose — to say she was sorry for the hurts she had caused him — and refraining from the accusatory "but you did such and such" statements.

She said that had been one of the most deeply touching moments of her life and that her husband had responded with a choked, "I'm sorry, too."

After that, she had no more nightmares in which she found herself back with him, being threatened or beaten and cringing in terror. The anger and resentment seemed to be totally eradicated. It wasn't churning within her and she seldom thought about the beatings or the more extensive store of resentments at the daily incidents of mental abuse which she had accepted and permitted to continue during the marriage.

She and her husband had occasional pleasant phone conversations about the children and a few hours of genuine communication when he came to their daughter's college graduation.

He was killed in an accident a year later and the woman said she was "so grateful that we had made our peace before he died."

A year or so later, when she began doing volunteer work at a shelter for battered wives she found, to her surprise, that, when one of the women would describe being beaten and abused, her own old hurt-anger surfaced again. She told the therapist, "I could feel it burning right under the skin of my chest and I would start compulsively trading 'abuse anecdotes' with the woman. I was not only surpised but I felt guilty that the anger was still there and was still so volatile."

This was when she contacted an anger therapist. She said she had long since realized that anger and resentment only hurt herself. She wanted to be rid of the anger but didn't know what else to do to finish it off.

It only took three sessions for her to complete it. Her previous general-counseling therapy after the divorce had been beneficial but had stopped short of helping her complete her angers because she never expressed them directly.

Even during the marriage, the beatings were never discussed between the couple and she didn't mention the situation to others until the last two years of the marriage.

When she had begun to tell others, it was done in the blaming mode: "He did this to me . . ." In her counseling after the divorce, she had merely related the incidents. In Anger Therapy, using the in-absentia technique, she began to express the anger with "I" language: "I resent you for . . .," "I hate you for . . ."

During the first session, the tears of hurt which had never been shed during the 15 years of marriage nor since, finally came. The dam was broken.

In the next session, she began taking control of the situation, telling her absent husband he was not going to control her anymore: "I resent your never taking me on a vacation or letting me have friends, and I'm not allowing you to interfere with my life anymore." She was also calling him names, yelling them at him and physically pounding out her anger on an overstuffed ottoman with a bataca: "Take that, you so and so. How do you like that, you . . . woman beater?" she demanded. Her yells turned into laughter with the release of the long pent-up emotion.

She left that session feeling exhilarated and "high." She had finally stood up for herself. In the third session, the therapist asked her if she was ready to bid her husband and the relationship goodbye. She said she was. She did an "appreciation and resentment" exercise, which allowed her to retain the memories of some good moments in the marriage without guilt at the other memories.

When she was finished, she spoke quietly and firmly to her husband, saying, "Thank you for being here with me. I hope you will be happy wherever you are but I am going on with my life. I don't need you anymore." She then covered the ottoman with a blanket and said, "Goodbye."

She told the therapist she had a mental image of her husband paddling off in a canoe around the bend of a mountain lake. The therapist asked, "How do you feel?"

In a quiet voice, she said, "Lonely. I don't have anyone to blame now."

That feeling soon passed and the "empty spaces inside" which she said she felt after release of the long-held and buried resentments were soon filled with positive feelings. Ridding the system of the anger cleared the spaces for new feelings of joy.

A few months later she called to tell the therapist her anger was "really, really gone." She said, "I know it's gone because I can listen to the stories from battered wives and even tell them enough of my own experience to give them the identification that is so important to them without being emotionally involved in those old incidents. I also no longer feel a need to go into blow-by-blow descriptions. Usually just a simple statement of history: 'I was a battered wife, too,' or 'That happened to me, too.' It *is* past history. This is freedom."

Help for Abusers

For the abuser, it is even more difficult to accept help and to do the work necessary to break the abuse cycle. But it can be done.

What makes it particularly difficult is that the abuser, too, is likely to have been abused as a child and so has all of that stored anger and hurt to work through plus the added burden of heavy guilt at now being an abuser.

Physical abusers who voluntarily seek help usually come to therapy in an extremely contrite state; mentally taking all the blame for the situation (although they may adopt a defensive pose if confronted outside of therapy). They feel "out of control" and helpless to do anything about their situation.

A wife batterer may be very apologetic the day after he has beaten his wife, full of remorse and saying, "I didn't really mean it." In this case, he has started to give the anger to his wife (during the beating) but then has taken it back afterward, retroflecting it to himself as guilt. In therapy, the person has to move past the guilt and own up to his anger so that he can work on releasing it.

The abusers who were either abused themselves as children or had mothers or sisters who were abused can't cope with the fact that, now, they are in the same category as the abusive person of their childhood. This thought is so repulsive to them, and is such a heavy self-judgment that they don't know how to begin to acknowledge it at a deep level. Usually, they have dealt with this thought by trying to brush it aside and thinking of something else.

Acknowledging and owning up to this fact takes more internal fortitude than anything else we have witnessed except for acknowledgment of sexual abuse by an abuser.

But the person must let himself (or herself) admit "ownership" of this fact and also let himself own it without whipping himself to death so he can grab hold of it and deal with the underlying anger.

This is not easy to effect because the abuser is in likelihood a person who has never learned to express or release emotions. The person is probably in the habit of "over-controlling" emotions, and fears that if he ever

starts releasing them — even in a therapeutically controlled environment — that he may never be able to
regain control.

Before therapy, the abuser is caught in a cyclic pattern which, at a subconscious level, follows this general
pattern: (1) Physical abuse of victim; (2) Guilt and fear
("Why did I do that" and "I'm scared to death I'm going
to kill her"); (3) Control ("The only way I can be sure I
won't kill her is to control every angry response I
have."); (4) Loss of control, "blowing up" again; (5)
Reinforcement of low self concept ("That proves it. I'm
sick. How could I beat someone I love? I'm out of
control.")

The abuser's belief that the only way to control (stop)
abusing is by not expressing emotion or anger is unreal-
istic because, one way or another, the emotion will out.
This over-control of the person's release system dam-
ages it, making it ultimately less effective than that of a
normal person. The over-controller has no way of releasing until the explosion.

We have never seen a case where a person who did
release anger in a safe, controlled situation in therapy
did not benefit from this. Rather than creating loss of
control, it returns the control to the person. If and
when the angers of years are completed one-by-one,
then the person no longer has a need to be an abuser.
This is analagous to the case of the man in the "Angry
Sex" chapter who, after releasing anger, said, "I guess
I don't need to be a premature ejaculator anymore."

But, in the case of abusers, professional work with a
trained Anger Therapist is definitely advised.

Childhood Sexual Abuse

Cases of childhood sexual abuse involve an even
more complicated mixture of feelings than do cases of

physical abuse. Here is a composite picture of feelings representative of many young girls who are abused sexually by fathers or other male caretakers: "I need the attention and Daddy is giving me the attention. I'm special . . . but something is wrong . . . I feel funny." (Sexual abuse of children by mothers or by older sisters also occurs but is not as common as abuse by men.)

This type of situation can be psychologically very seductive to a child. She needs love and a male seems to be giving her love but the "funny" feelings are there as well.

As the child grows older and develops a sense of the societal norms for right and wrong, she picks up guilt but is still "into" the situation. And, if the male, so often the father, is "loving" in this relationship rather than merely physically demanding, it becomes even more difficult for the girl to separate and sort out her feelings.

In many cases, even after the person is grown and out of the scenario, it is almost impossible for her to cut a path through the other emotions to get to the anger.

If she was a "willing" participant, she frequently feels, "What is there to be angry about?" If she was physically forced, she is apt to feel, as did the physically abused child, that she was "not very smart" or she should have known how to deal with it in a better way.

Another common feeling is that there is something wrong with her or it wouldn't have happened to her in the first place. Because, typically, she has never shared this part of her history, she may not know of other cases in which this has happened and thinks it doesn't happen to nice people.

Guilt may also exist both at the time the situation is active and later. At the time, she may feel, "Maybe this is happening because of my way of acting."

Mothers can foster this feeling. Those who are aware of incestuous relationships between their husbands and

daughters but choose to "turn their heads" not uncom-
monly accuse the child, by look or implication, of being
seductive to the father, stepfather, uncle or man in
question. At best, they may do nothing to stop the
situation, creating another source of deep hurt and
anger that the child carries throughout life.

In fact, the anger at the "innocent" parent can be
even harder to deal with than anger at the abuser. In
adulthood, it may become obvious to the victim that the
abuser was "sick." But what about the mother who
"stood by and let me be treated that way?"

If the sexual abuse of a child continues over any
length of time, the mother almost certainly knows of it,
at least senses it. The telltale signs will be there: the
exchanged glances, the secretive gestures. These
mothers may find it easier to ignore and deny the
situation than to confront it.

Perhaps they fear they will lose their husband or
boyfriend and have to support themselves or be left
without a man. Perhaps it frees them from having to
have sex with the man themselves. Perhaps they just
find it easier to look the other way.

An Incest Victim

One young woman came for counseling after reading
an article on Anger Therapy in which incest was mentioned. She was a highly productive, successful individual who was enjoying her social life as well as her career.
This was how she described herself, and there was
nothing in her appearance or actions that belied this.

She got right to the point: "I want to deal with the
fact that I was a victim of incest as a child. My father
now lives in another city and I feel that what happened
is all in the past.

"But when I read that article I began to realize what a tremendous influence it has on my life — on my social and personal relationships, on my career, on my attitudes about marriage, about having children, about being around other people's children — and I want to be free of that influence.

"I want to be able to make healthy, free choices about my future and I don't want this cropping up later on."

Despite her willingness, it was extremely hard for her to admit to her rage at her father because he had been one of the more "loving" incestuous fathers.

In order to cleanse her system of the negative effects of the early experiences, she had to acknowledge her right to be enraged, even though she did love him. She thought that if she admitted she had ever hated him it would mean she had quit loving him.

She agreed to do an *in absentia* chair encounter with him, in which she expressed her anger: "I hate you for what you did to me. I was a child and you took me at a point when I didn't have the knowledge or the maturity or the ability to stand up to you.

"I am angry because you talked me into believing it was OK. It wasn't OK and something inside me kept saying, 'It's not OK,' because I wasn't happy. But I needed you and I was afraid I'd lose your love. I hate you for that terrible manipulation of my feelings and my trust."

In one hour she was able to fully complete that anger and by the time the session was over she had let herself feel the rage, the hurt. She had cried and had truly put that experience in the past. Releasing the anger also released her feelings of guilt at having the anger.

When we say experiences can be put in the past, we do not mean they are forgotten. Rather, they become healed wounds which we know were once open and festering but which no longer cause intense pain.

Rape and Homicide

Rape is another abuse which is now widely recognized to be an act of violence rather than a crime of sex. We consider it to be a form of homicide, an act of psychotic fury. The enormity of rape or even actual homicide is beyond the scope and available space of this book except to note that victims of rape can benefit tremendously from Anger Therapy in the same manner as victims of other abuses.

Suicide

Barring homicide, suicide is the ultimate angry act. In fact, the person who commits suicide usually "kills" two people: himself or herself and the person they usually want to "show" or "make sorry."

Among other things, suicides turn their rage at another person or their hostility at the world back on themselves, but the emotions and dynamics involved in suicide cannot be delineated in simplistic terms. It is one of the most complex of all anger games and the one in which it is obviously impossible to obtain information from the perpetrator unless the suicide attempt failed.

Our experience with persons in therapy who had made unsuccessful suicide attempts, and with persons who were survivors in a loved one's successful suicide, attest to the strong involvement of anger.

Another aspect of suicide is that it is a manipulative device. Instead of confronting their anger, suicides, in effect, turn their backs on it and leave the "mess," whatever it may be, for others to contend with.

This is an extreme way to avoid confrontation, to avoid coping. It's also a very effective way of "getting even," of saying, "OK, let's see how you handle it. Now, you can worry about the bills, or the kids, or junior's drug problem, or your mother's need for a home."

One of the objectives of the suicide is to heap guilt on those who are left behind and this usually does happen. Even in normal death, survivors experience degrees of guilt, feeling they should have "done more" or "been better." When the death is by suicide, this is magnified or multiplied many times over.

This is what the suicidal person thought would happen: "I'll show you. I'll blow my brains out (or take a pill overdose) and then maybe you'll be sorry you were such a bad wife, husband, child" or "You'll be sorry you didn't give me more attention and love."

Even if the suicidal person does not have feelings such as these — which is unlikely — this is the message which the person left behind receives. To have a parent or a spouse commit suicide is usually taken as the ultimate form of rejection. The survivor is left with a great deal of anger: "Why didn't he/she discuss it (the problem) with me?"; "What could have been so terrible that we couldn't have worked it out together?"; "Why didn't he/she trust me?"; "Why did she/he leave me?"; "How could he/she have done this to me?"

Yet, it is not socially "nice" to get angry at dead persons. So most survivors repress their anger and get caught in the grief (which they also feel) instead.

In therapy, the objective is to help survivors move past feeling aghast, responsible and guilty to a place where they can face the fact that they do have anger.

Grief Abuse

In one family in which the father had committed suicide, all the family members but one had moved past a normal grieving period into being able to think of and talk about the father in a realistic manner.

The father had been a practicing alcoholic with many of the negative characteristics and actions common to alcoholism and addiction. He had also had many good traits and had done numerous loving things. This reality of the love and anger felt by the family had been fairly well put into a healthy perspective by all but the 15-year-old son who, three years after the suicide, was unwilling to move out of active grief, defensive grief.

When one of the other members would mention in passing one of the less than admirable actions of the father, this son would come quickly to his father's defense: "Poor old Dad, how can you talk about him that way? He was doing the best he could. Maybe if we had appreciated him more, he wouldn't have had to kill himself. Maybe we drove him to it."

In situations such as this, the anger therapist helps the person identify and confront the anger. In this case, it came out in therapy that the son was, indeed, angry, actually furious at the way he had been treated by his father.

The father had been away from home a great deal and when he was home he was verbally abusive. The son needed love and attention from his father but what he felt was absence and abuse. As an adolescent, he was unable to deal with his anger at that treatment and, since Dad was so seldom home, he used that time to try to get in Dad's good graces.

That didn't work so he turned to drugs to anesthetize the hurt-anger. When the father killed himself, he fantasized that his relationship with Dad had been a loving one. He couldn't acknowledge his anger because, in his mind, that would have meant saying that his father really hadn't cared for him, and he couldn't bear to deal with that possibility. Instead, he kept the fantasy going, defending his father unrealistically, and staying in the grief.

This might be called grief abuse because, although he did have genuine grief, it had been carried on in an active stage far beyond its capacity to clear the system.

Now, the anger was attempting to come out but, instead, the grief was prolonged.

When this son worked out his anger in therapy, he was able to move past the grief and also to realize that his anger was as valid as his love for his father. They are both valid emotions and one feeling does not cancel out the other.

The whole family participated in group therapy and members were able to work out past problems and current family relationships. For some, it took more work and a longer time to achieve hoped-for results but, in all cases, they said they benefitted from the experience.

Suicide is such a traumatic experience to survivors that, without help of some kind, it is unlikely those wounds will ever really become clean scars, closed and completed incidents. In therapy, we have seen many people who had literally been grieving for years deal with their anger and move past the grief.

One man who came for therapy about another situation mentioned that his former wife had committed suicide. He said, "When I walked into the house and saw her dead on the floor from an overdose of pills, I kicked her and called her a name."

That may not be the expected or socially accepted way of dealing with a suicide but it may have been a much more healthy and honest reaction than those we usually witness.

Among persons who have sought therapy after unsuccessful suicide attempts there is, again, much anger to be dealt with. The suicide syndrome is not irreversible — until the act has been committed.

Releasing the anger connected with any of the abuse experiences described in this chapter or with less severe forms of the abuses is possible through the exercises whether or not the person is present and whether or not the person is still alive. This release is necessary in order to move on to the possibility of living life at its full potential.

EXERCISES

Exercise 1. My Response Was the Right One at the Time.

Sit quietly with yourself and remember a time as a child when you were frightened by someone who was older, bigger, stronger, meaner. Remember how you responded and how that response affected the situation. Did it stop the other person or in some way protect your well being?

Take a sheet of paper and on the left half list your responses as a child to being abused, such as crying, hiding, going along with the action, and so on. Then, on the right half of the paper, list all of the benefits of that behavior such as "The hitting or shouting stopped" or "The other person left the room" or "They couldn't find me."

After you have completed the list of behaviors and results, take a few minutes to think of what would have happened to you if you had not taken such action. Now, write three different notes to yourself, congratulating or thanking yourself for actions which were appropriate at the time.

Exercise 2. Low Self-Concept.

Make a list of all the sentences you have said to yourself about how inadequate you are as a person, such as: "I am not likeable," "Anybody can tell me what to do," "I am nobody without . . .," "I can't do it," "I'll probably fail."

Now, trace back in your life and notice when each of these became part of your self messages. How many date back to the days when (if) you were abused as a child?

Exercise 3. Suicidal Tendencies.

When did you last have a thought regarding suicide? Remember what was happening in your life right before the suicidal thoughts. See if there is any connection between the suicidal thoughts and the suppression of anger or hurt.

Exercise 4. Suicide of Another.

Remember when someone you know made a suicide threat to you. How did you respond at the moment? Do you remember any anger or was there just fear, or sympathy or protective feelings? How do you feel now about the suicide threat?

Exercise 5. Releasing the Anger.

Select and practice the anger-release exercises learned in previous chapters, focusing on situations of abuse.

9

THE ANGER COMPONENT IN PAIN AND DISEASE

There is a growing body of information and knowledge that shows a definite link between the way we feel (or don't allow ourselves to feel) emotionally and the way we feel physically. The hurts or angers that we don't express can manifest as physical hurts (pain) or bodily "angers" (infections of endless variety and even diseases).

This knowledge about the relationship of physical conditions to emotions, particularly anger, falls into two categories.

The first category is experiential, or empirical, knowledge. This is knowledge that is gained directly from clients and patients, either from their subjective self-reporting — telling in their own words how they feel before and after the healthy expression of anger — or from therapists or family members who observe the physical changes clients undergo during and after Anger Therapy.

The second category involves data obtained from planned and carefully controlled and monitored research studies conducted with selected groups of subjects. The data are carefully measured, compared and interpreted in studies of this kind.

In this chapter we will present examples from both categories.

Bleeding Ulcer

In the first category is the case of a schoolteacher with a bleeding ulcer of the colon who was referred to an anger therapist by her physician.

For several years, she had been unable to fulfill her contract with the school district because, each year, she had required hospital treatment plus additional time off to recuperate.

She had remarkably quick results with the anger therapy and reported to the therapist that the bleeding of the ulcer had stopped after only one session. She said she had been retested by her physician who found no sign of the ulcer.

This woman's husband had been killed in Vietnam. While he was away, she had had an extramarital affair and, when she learned he had been killed, she was overcome with guilt.

In the session with the therapist, the guilt came out as anger — anger at her husband for having gone off and left her, thus causing her loneliness which, in turn, led to the affair (anger is often not logical). When she got rid of the anger, she got rid of the guilt — and the ulcer.

Eczema

In the anger workshops, students always do anger work of their own as well as learning the principles of Anger Therapy and it was after one of these sessions that a 36-year-old in a graduate-level workshop reported a breakthrough with anger that directly affected her skin condition.

She said, "As far back as I can remember, I have had very bad eczema." The eczema was mainly on her arms, accompanied by occasional "flare-ups" on other parts of her body, she reported.

She had gone to "countless dermatologists" and tried many different creams and oral medications. "Nothing seemed to work," she said. "Sometimes the rash was controlled, but not for any duration."

Following the work-out session, she reported how words and feelings started to come out and "exploded from me."

She told how, during the session, she had worked on the abuse — beatings — inflicted on her by her mother when she was a child.

"The small hallway where it occurred (all came back) and I centered on my mother's hands."

She said that after the session she felt "a great sense of relief and uplifting" and she reported that "shortly after the (anger) work, my hands cleared up — with no creams, no oral medications."

For two years previously, she said, the eczema had been so severe that she couldn't bend her fingers without "the skin cracking and bleeding."

This woman had done her anger work in the spring of that year and, by December, the eczema had not returned. "My hands are perfect," she wrote to the therapist, "and I have no eczema anywhere. This is the longest I have ever gone without some kind of flare-up."

She reported that she had also been able to establish a loving relationship with her mother after the anger work, which had not been possible before.

Chronic Sinusitis

One client, who was nearing 40 when he sought help in one-to-one therapy, saw his long-standing sinus condition healed when he worked out anger at his parents — at his father for committing suicide and at his mother for incidents of sexual abuse in his childhood.

He self-reported the results, noting that when he worked on the suicide — which had occurred 11 years previously — he mentally went into the room again where his father's "brains were splattered on the ceiling and walls by the shotgun blast."

He continued, "I worked through that and had the first sense of relief and freedom I had since rare moments as a child.

"One of the side effects of that first session, and of a later one where I worked on (anger at) my mother, was a healing of badly infected sinuses."

During both sessions, he reported hearing "a popping in my head that was so loud I asked the therapist if he heard it."

Multiple Ailments

Another male patient, who was 45 when he was referred to Anger Therapy, said he had been treated for numerous maladies over a period of many years, with symptoms seeming to increase rather than be relieved. He even had to give up his profession as a pilot because of his many ailments and because of fear, tenseness and lack of confidence.

The first symptom, "cervical pain in the neck," had appeared 10 years earlier, he said, and was diagnosed three years after that as neurosis. He reported, "I had severe tension headaches at that time, severe pain in the cervical and shoulder areas to the point of not being able to drive."

The following year, he received a diagnosis of cervical spondylitis and osteoarthritis in both the cervical and the lower spine, he said, and went to a natural hot springs resort for treatment.

Two years later, he had additional symptoms: severe intestinal cramps and an inability to urinate. He was checked for hernia, with none found, and had urine samples tested, with no negative results.

He said, "I started having severe diarrhea problems and problems of losing focus in my eyes. The arthritic problems were increasing in the lower back, making it difficult to walk."

He also started having skin eruptions and "many boil-like configurations." He underwent complete allergy testing and was declared non-allergic.

This man said that the next year an endocrinologist told him he had gross glandular problems and did find a duodenal ulcer — but nothing else to explain his diarrhea, excessive gas, low blood sugar, dizziness, and the problems with focusing his eyes.

"The doctor diagnosed psychosomatic illness . . . and initiated Anger Therapy," he said.

In a taped report by the patient, made after his third one-hour Anger Therapy session, he reported many of the minute details of his improved condition, including, "less nervousness — chest feels more relaxed, easier to breathe — shallow breath and tightness is gone. No feeling of heaviness in abdominal area. More stamina in legs . . . eyes clear, focusing much better, feel more alert."

He also reported improved physical coordination, citing details of his golf game and swimming sessions with an instructor.

And the ulcer healed. "If it's there, I'm not aware of it. I eat most everything. Skin is (also) cleared up completely."

This man's anger, released in therapy, dated back to childhood when he had been fearful — for himself and for his younger sister — of his physically abusive mother.

The father had left home and his mother was raising him and his sister. He remembered that when his mother, who had a drinking problem, was on a "drinking rampage," he and his sister would hide under the bed.

When the therapist asked him to reenact the scene, he curled up on the floor. "I remember her coming at us, reaching under the bed with the broom. She was screaming. I was always trying to protect my sister. I would hold my hand over her mouth so she wouldn't make any noise, telling her we had to become invisible."

As the man relived this scene, his body became extremely tense and he was hovering over the imaged figure of his little sister.

The emotions connected with these incidents were never dealt with and had lingered in his body, seeking to express themselves through a variety of physical ailments. The never-released tenseness had finally made him so tense he couldn't fly anymore.

Even when the mind manages to forget such emotional traumas, the body remembers.

After the third therapy session, he reported, "All physical symptoms (are) either dissipated or in a reduced state — more confidence, less fear, more understanding with family, better tolerance with wife."

Mental Illness

Some patients with mental illness — which is often believed to be caused by or linked to a biochemical, that is, physical, imbalance — have also achieved relief of symptoms through directed expression of anger.

One woman who was diagnosed as schizophrenic experienced dramatic results from the same kind of anger-release exercises we have been discussing throughout this book, as did a man who was diagnosed as manic-depressive.

Following are excerpts from these clients' written self-reports:

Schizophrenic Woman

This woman wrote in her self-report: "Anger nearly killed me. A suicide attempt at 18 began a spiral of violence, depression, self-mutilation and 'mad-ness' that hospitalized me in a psychiatric ward with a diagnosis of 'schizophrenic.'"

She reported that she spent nearly two years "playing the hospital game, acting out in whatever ways upset the staff the most."

She continued, "I entered into 'sickness' with all the energy I could muster. Since I was considered 'sick and dangerous,' I was determined to be the sickest, craziest patient imaginable.

"It was obvious that everyone was terrified of my anger and this frightened me into forcing the staff to confine me so I spent most of the time in the classical 'bare room,' often restrained and heavily sedated."

For months, she refused to talk, made repeated suicide attempts, escaped, threw food and mutilated herself with contraband glass or razors, and beat her hands on the wall, she said.

"This came to an end only when I was told that I would shortly be committed to the state hospital," she said.

"I was terrified that, once inside there, I would be locked up for life — and some marvelously healthy part of me did not want that!

"I changed my behavior radically and went obediently to occupational therapy to weave placemats until I was considered 'well' enough to leave."

When she left the hospital, she was able to function, supported by continuous psychotherapy, drugs and the positive effect of an emotionally sustaining job, she said. She added that "the basic problems, however, were not dealt with and continued to limit my life.

"I learned a succession of defenses which allowed me to function and which kept me out of the hospital, and I resigned myself to a barely manageable half-life for a number of years.

"But I believe now that all this time I was moving toward health as I became more and more unhappy with the limitations under which I had placed myself in order to function."

A friend suggested Gestalt Therapy (with the Anger Therapist featured here) which she began "with much trepidation."

Explaining her fear in her report, she said, "Although I was not as I wished, I was very afraid of rocking the boat and driving myself back into some non-functioning, 'crazy' state."

In her first meeting with the therapist, she was reassured that, "You will not be unable to function unless you want to be unable."

That response was "the beginning of freedom" for her, she said, "the freedom to be responsible for my own life and for everything I did.

"It was the absolute end of 'victim,' 'patient,' 'sickness' and the beginning of power, the real power to choose and to be responsible for every choice I made.

"As I gave up helplessness, I began to trust myself to feel what I was feeling and to know that I could survive it.

"I had finally found a therapist who was not afraid of my anger and who did not try to confine or drug me."

Reporting that she spent many hours "letting the old angers go," she said she found the rage she had feared for so long was not overwhelming or deadly "once it was expressed in the therapeutic situation."

She said that "after years of 'talking about' the anger, I was struck by the immediate relief and radical change which occurred after physically expressing it."

She referred to the anger work as "the beginning of owning so much of myself which had been denied."

Summing up the results of the therapy, she wrote, "The most important change was a trust in my own organism — learning that I always move toward health and growth if I just stay out of my own way!

"Now, when I want to beat on the bed, I do it. Anger is more burden than I am willing to carry for very long. The same with tears and other miseries. I've come to rely on my own intuitive knowing for what I need.

"I feel truly free to risk, to change, to live the minutes one at a time wide open."

Chronically Depressed Man

A man who wrote to the anger therapist a couple of months after his first Anger Therapy session said he wanted to "put my experiences into perspective and relate these to you in writing."

He said he had the "typical background of a chronically depressed individual."

Other members of his immediate family had been diagnosed as depressed, he said, adding that, "on the whole, every member of the family is 'emotionally constipated'."

He said it was a family pattern to handle emotions "by withdrawal."

When he himself was in a state of withdrawal during an extremely stressful period, a concerned friend urged him to go to a doctor, which he did, and he began taking anti-depressive medication.

He hated the idea of taking the pills, he said, because he equated this dependence with mental illness. He said he realized that "a pill, or a hundred pills, could not change my self-destructive behavior," and he stopped taking them.

"Soon the anxiety and depression could not be held at bay any longer and returned. My agony was now complete. I could either be depressed for the rest of my life or take drugs the rest of my life. I chose to make my life as short as possible and kill myself."

After a nearly successful suicide attempt that sent him first to an emergency hospital and then to a psychiatric hospital, the man experienced a reversal of attitude. He said, "My full intention from the first day in the hospital after I regained consciousness was to get out as soon as possible and then to find, in my own way, something worth living for."

He said he was "resolved to do whatever was necessary to get where I wanted to be."

This client was treated in the psychiatric hospital both with drugs to control his mood swings and by seeing a psychiatrist. When he was released from the hospital, he was taken off the drugs, and said that "for the next three months, the only way I got through each day was by reminding myself that I didn't want to die, that I really wanted to live."

When a friend suggested Anger Therapy, he said he was resistant to the suggestion "because nothing could have been less in line with what I was thinking or what I wanted to pursue."

Nevertheless, he did call for an appointment, reporting the remembered incident later in his letter to the therapist: "When I spoke to you over the telephone, the tension was unbearable . . . I was desperate and had absolutely no faith."

By the time he arrived for the first appointment, he said, his anxiety "had reached levels unknown to me before.

"I remember telling you that I wanted to leave and you gave me permission to go.

"At that point, I made the decision, probably for the first time in my life, to participate in something fully. This time it was in my own mental health. I remember our discussion about guilt, depression and anger almost verbatim."

When the man was asked if he wanted to do some work on his anger, he said he "decided to trust another human being as I had never done before."

He recalled that he had chosen his father as the first subject for his anger work because, "I wanted to start slowly and I could not describe any feelings toward my father, only ambivalence, certainly not anger.

"Boy, was I surprised! When you gave me permission to express the anger I felt toward him, it was as though a dam broke inside of me. I could feel the eruption of anger and it poured and poured, and poured out.

"In the distance, I could hear your voice, encouraging, reassuring. You directed me through some mindlessly simple exercises and for the first time I felt something toward my father.

"I wanted to kill him for having neglected me. Instead, I had been killing myself.

"After the anger had been vented, I felt all of the love I had wanted to express for so long. It felt complete. I could breathe deeply. The air was sweet, and still is. My shoulders relaxed, my stomach filled with air. It was totally, entirely and completely delightful feeling the 'flowing' of energy through my body."

The man reported that his life then began to take on more meaning and that, although all of his problems with money or with relationships were not solved, there was now "action where there was immobility, trust in myself where there was despair.

". . . Up until recently, I defined my life as 'not dying.' But a few weeks ago, as I was showering, I realized that now I was simply 'living' and I broke into tears. I could never have done that before. My life now requires no motive.

". . . I realize that in a few weeks, or months, the problems of an entire life cannot be solved, but I believe that I have taken a great stride toward living my life."

These cases are from hundreds encountered in clinical practice; the literature abounds with thousands of similar case histories.

Scientific Studies

Scientifically controlled studies, as indicated earlier, are long-term projects. They require painstaking collection and analysis of data.

For a study to be termed scientific, it must have a hypothesis (working premise), a research design (a planned course of action for controlled testing), a specifically selected group of subjects, and reliable evaluation components that are built into its design.

Usually, if preliminary experimental testing supports the hypothesis, a small pilot study is undertaken in which subjects are carefully chosen to eliminate variable factors such as age, sex and health history.

If results of the pilot study are still supportive of the hypothesis, larger studies are done and, finally, the study must be replicated by other scientists with other control groups in other parts of the country to see if the same results accrue.

This must be done numerous times, usually over a period of many years, before the hypothesis is accepted as a proven theory.

Preliminary reports of studies on the relationship between emotions and illness are now appearing frequently, even in the popular press.

A January, 1983, Associated Press (AP) wire story, datelined Boston, reported on several studies linking cancer to personality. It cited studies being conducted at Harvard Medical School by a psychologist and cell biologist, by scientists at Rush-Presbyterian-St. Luke's Medical Center in Chicago, by a scientist at Johns Hopkins University in Baltimore and by physicians at King's College Hospital in London. One study cited in the article had been ongoing since 1948.

Among findings reported were these: People with the "cancer personality" tend to be quiet, placid, emotionally repressed people who do not express their negative emotions and, in fact, have difficulty expressing any feelings.

One of the studies showed that the subjects were people who, when something bad happened to them, did "not blow up in anger or fight back."

The story noted that psychologists first began to consider attributes of a cancer personality after measuring the attitudes of people who already had cancer. Newer studies have measured personalities among disease-free groups of people, following the subjects over a period of many years in order to correlate personality traits with those who did or did not contract cancer at a later period.

In one such study, a personality test was administered to 2,020 men and when follow-up was done 17 years later, it was found that those who had shown depression on their early tests were twice as likely to have died from cancer.

In the London research, doctors studied 160 women who were admitted for biopsy of breast lumps. They found "more suppression of anger on those whose lumps turned out to be cancerous."

One scientist quoted in the story noted that cancer survivors may be difficult patients to work with because they do not readily comply but, instead, question all procedures and voice complaints. He pointed out, though, that, "They do much better than the nice, compliant sort of person(s) who can't seem to express their anger at all."

In the October, 1981, issue of Glamour magazine a story on eating disorders reported on several studies, one of which showed that women with bulimia (binge/ vomit eating disorder) displayed more irritability, sadness and loneliness than a control group of women with "normal" eating behaviors who were used for comparison. The scientist added, "We also found more anger more frequently in the bulimics."

As part of the information gathering process during the study, some of the bulimic women carried beepers over the course of a week. The research staff beeped the women every few hours at unspecified times, at which times the women would stop what they were doing and record — on a series of rating scales contained in diaries — their moods, thoughts and behavior at that moment.

The diary entries were then fed into a computer for analysis. Many of the subjects were beeped mid-binge or mid-purge and the researcher reported, "During the binge, there is a signficant spike of anger. During the purge, the anger is relieved to the point of nearly flattening out. After the purge, the anger reverts to a level just slightly lower than before the binge."

Studies testing the emotion-disease relationship are also being published with increasing frequency in medical and scientific journals. A study conducted by three scientists at the University of Arizona College of Medicine compared men obsessed with long-distance running to women who starve themselves with incessant, inordinate dieting (anorexics). Their report appeared in the 1983 issue of the prestigious New England Journal of Medicine.

The researchers had interviewed 60 long-distance runners and found many similarities between obsessive runners and the women with anorexia. Among the similarities was the fact that both tended to be "compliant, self-effacing and uncomfortable with the direct expression of anger."

Anger and Arthritis Study

The motivation for a scientific study conducted by the anger therapist featured in this book came during a private therapy session with a man who was seeking help in working out his unhappy relationship with his mother.

In the session, he was verbalizing the unexpressed anger of decades, expressing it directly to his mother, who was symbolically placed in the empty chair facing him.

Telling his mother how he felt "face-to-face" was serving to process his long-stored anger. His emotion mounted as he hurled the litany of smothered resentments at her and he finally focused on her characteristic of never expressing emotion.

Then came the spontaneous and incisive burst of words: "I resent you for taking all your anger and freezing it in those arthritic joints."

The man was able to complete his own stored anger at his mother, and the therapist was motivated to begin work on long-considered scientific studies on the relationship between anger and pain and anger and disease.

He launched the research project with several colleagues, including other psychologists, the director of a university pain clinic and other anger therapists.

The first two phases of the study involved the testing of a group of pain clinic patients and a controlled pilot study of six women with rheumatoid arthritis. The latter phase was funded by a donor through the Southwest Arthritis Foundation in Tucson.

During the first phase, with the pain patients, a group therapy session was videotaped. There was also subjective patient-reporting, and there was psychological testing by the scientists, who also recorded their clinical observations of the subjects.

One woman in the group, who was in her forties, volunteered to do the first piece of anger work. She had been suffering with chronic back pain for 16 years and had been a semi-invalid for many years. At the time of the therapy session (the first of eight group sessions), she said no previous treatment had been effective in alleviating her pain although she had tried various drug therapies as well as physical therapy.

She explained to the group that her husband helped her to function by physically assisting her navigation and waiting on her. Because of his long-term continuing assistance, and because he had stayed with her, she had made up her mind that she had no right or justification to become angry at her husband.

At the same time, she was enraged at her dependence on him and also resentful of his ability to do whatever he chose to do physically. She felt guilt about her resentment: "How could I be angry at such a kind and gentle soul?"

The husband, on the other hand, it was later learned, had built up his own store of unresolved resentments because of all the extra work her condition caused and because of being tied down to a semi-invalid.

He, too, felt guilt at his anger. He reported later that he would frequently ask himself, "How can you get angry at someone who is ill and can't help what she is going through?"

Both were stuck in their resentments toward the other and their relationship was suffering the consequences of the unresolved feelings.

In the course of the 45-minute group therapy session, the woman was able to acknowledge to herself that she had anger and to express it out loud to her husband symbolically.

In the final stages of the session, she beat vigorously on a large ottoman with a bataca (the bat-like anger-release "tool") as she yelled, "Sick in the stomach, sick in the head, sick in my joints, sick everywhere, just because I wasn't willing to show you how angry I am."

This woman — with chronic back pain so severe she could barely walk — was beating the ottoman as if she were a lumberjack chopping wood.

The videotape documented her physical transformation and also recorded the change in her voice from whiny to clear and forceful.

Prior to the session, the woman had rated her pain (on a self-report chart with pain-intensity designations of 1 to 100) at 85.

When she was asked to rate it after the session, she said, "Zero." The therapist said, "That would mean you don't have any pain." She responded, "I said 'zero' and I mean 'zero.'"

This dramatic breakthrough was accomplished despite the fact that there was much more external pressure than in a normal group therapy session because of the videotaping lights, the presence of the taping crew and the monitoring by the researchers.

The woman had never engaged in Anger Therapy before and had no preconceived ideas about it.

After the session, she made a contract with herself to start expressing her emotions and she also asked to have the videotape shown to her husband. When he came in to view it, he commented, "I was wondering how long it would be before you got that out."

Progress of other pain patients participating in this study varied, apparently depending on their commitment to the therapy. Overall, results were supportive of the scientists' hypothesis, so they proceeded to the next phase, the more tightly controlled pilot study.

Arthritic Patients

In this phase, the study was narrowed to testing of six women with rheumatoid arthritis. The hypothesis was: The expression or suppression of anger has a direct relationship to the control of pain and disease, specifically arthritic pain.

Prior to commencing, the scientists conducted library research on studies of arthritis done over a 50-year period. This search revealed common characteristics among arthritics, notably that, traditionally, they have submissive, compliant personalities.

They were shown to be people who have difficulty expressing emotional reactions, especially in the area of hostility. It was also shown that the majority had an unresolved relationship with a parental figure.

Women were chosen for the pilot study because statistics indicated that women with arthritis outnumbered men with the condition five-to-one or up to 20-to-one, depending on the reports consulted.

The six women selected had all been tested and diagnosed by a certified rheumatologist to be in an advanced stage of rheumatoid arthritis — which involves severe crippling — but not in a state beyond which change could be accomplished.

A four-week baseline period, in which tests were administered and questionnaires answered, preceded 10 weeks of once-a-week individual therapy for each patient.

The findings of the study were that five of the six patients reported improvement.

The most radical improvement was demonstrated by a woman in her early 30s. Three sessions in particular were notable, the three where she most actively involved herself in the therapy.

During the course of these sessions, she showed a significant drop in scores rating depression, hostility, psychoticism (feelings of being fragmented, scattered, and so on) and her self-evaluation of pain also dropped — 38 percent in one session.

One of the productive sessions involved her identification and expression of anger at her mother. With her mother in the empty chair, the woman began expressing herself to her mother until she got to her feelings. The therapist's report indicated that most of the session was unemotional until this point — even though the woman had acknowledged having pain in the back of her head and in her spine.

When she did get to the feelings, there were tears first and then anger. She said to her mother, "I won't scare me about you anymore." She reported that the pain left her spine at the point she made the statement and she said she felt "relaxed," "fantastic," "good" and now more ready to speak with her mother directly in real life.

After the three productive sessions, there was one in which the therapist reported her anger work as "sluggish" and lacking in direction. He noted that her release of emotion during this session was "questionable" and her self-report of the session showed her pain levels had gone up again.

However, at the end of 10 weeks of therapy, she reported having learned: to get her emotions out; to finish relationships, either in person or symbolically; that "emotions relate to relaxation"; that she felt less pain; and that she was less dependent on medication.

Certain uncontrollable variables entered into this study: one patient developed a kidney infection which necessitated antibiotics and thus changed her medical regimen (all patients were originally on identical drug regimens during the study); another subject experienced trauma from a death in the family; the Tucson winter was more severe than usual; and one woman became pregnant.

Uncontrollable variables such as these are one reason human studies are complicated and long-term and why replication of the research with a number of groups is necessary.

A Directional Change

In this Tucson study, however, despite the uncontrollable variables, there was definitely a directional change — and it was a change in the right direction.

Following this pilot study, the National Institute of Mental Health (NIMH) funded a two-year study by the same principal investigators to test the effect of Anger Therapy on depression and on intensity and duration of pain among 20 psychogenic pain patients who had little or no physical basis for their pain and who also suffered from depression.

As this book goes to press, the study is not complete; the data have yet to be analyzed and the scientific results must be tabulated. But personal feedback from these patients with psychogenic pain — traditionally among the hardest patients to treat — was often very positive.

These studies and many others across the country are giving and will increasingly provide the scientific corroboration of the beneficial results of Anger Therapy on pain and disease. In the meantime, patients who have already experienced these positive results have their own corroboration.

10

ANGER THERAPY

Through the pages of this book, you have attended therapy sessions and witnessed real people with bottled-up anger learn to release it and move on to more productive, more fulfilling lives. If you have done the exercises, you should have experienced the positive results of the techniques in your own life.

It is not necessary to understand the concepts, theoretical constructs and dynamics of Anger Therapy in order for it to work for you but most of us are interested in knowing the hows and the whys of things that are important to us. It is also reassuring to learn more about the scientific underpinnings of a therapy in which we become involved.

We have seen that the first step in any type of healthy anger work is becoming willing to tackle the work. So, let's consider some of the common excuses people use for not dealing with anger. If you have experienced feelings of resistance to working the various exercises, you've probably already encountered some of these in yourself.

Excuses

1. I don't have any anger.

2. There's no need to work on it; it was in the past.

3. It's not significant.

4. I can now understand why he/she did it; that should solve it.

5. The other party won't listen, or won't understand.

6. If I deal with my anger, I'll drive people away from me; they won't love me anymore. He/she will leave the relationship.

7. I'll hurt somebody (emotionally or physically).

8. I'll be hurt (emotionally or physically).

9. I won't be able to stand the pain of dredging up all that old business.

10. I've tried to vent anger before; it only made me feel worse.

11. I'm not going to let that so-and-so off the hook; I'm going to stay angry a little longer.

We've already seen how deceptive, and erroneous, the "I don't have any anger" excuse is, and also how the rationalization that "it's in the past" or "it's insignificant" doesn't mean a thing if the pain still exists in the present.

The attempt to intellectualize the anger also doesn't work. "Understanding" the other person's reason for hurting us such as: "He was emotionally disturbed himself" or "She didn't know it mattered to me" doesn't heal the pain or get rid of the anger. The human system doesn't respond to rationalization or intellectualizing, only to what it is feeling.

The fear that the other person won't listen seldom materializes when put to the test. It is rare that another person won't listen to non-combative revelations of true feelings.

The fear that expression of anger will drive another away also doesn't prove out — if we are expressing in a clean, direct manner. In fact, it is the non-expression or repression of anger that is much more likely to eventually drive the other person away because the anger will out and it will out in more insidious ways.

Emotionally or physically hurting another can be avoided by using the exercises to release the anger in private, taking the venom and sting out of it before expressing it in person.

When the anger is truly completed and finished in therapy, it no longer exists as a volatile entity and the dangerous tendencies bred by stored anger are dissipated with its release.

The fear of being hurt is another matter. As we emphasized in the chapter on anger and abuse, this fear is very possibly based on the reality of past physical abuse from the other party and we do not recommend direct confrontation. However, the anger can still be released in therapy or through the exercises.

The excuse that "I won't be able to stand the pain" is usually discarded when the pain of not dealing with the anger becomes more unbearable than the anxiety about dealing.

The person who says, "I've tried it before, and it doesn't work," has probably been using an ineffective method of expressing such as blaming or complaining which, indeed, do not serve to complete the anger nor to provide relief.

Not wanting to let the other person "off the hook" is an excuse which most people find very difficult to admit, but it is common. Remember the battered wife who completed old anger at her ex-husband? When the therapist asked her how she felt, she said, "Lonely. I don't have anyone to blame now." There is also a revenge factor involved, a feeling that our active anger is somehow "paying back" the hurt the other party caused us.

It is admittedly difficult to move past the excuses. It takes courage because acknowledgment of the anger signals breaking up the game that has become familiar.

There is risk involved because, although a familiar situation or way of dealing may be miserable and non-productive, it is known, while change represents the unknown. But the anger must be acknowledged for the productive work to begin.

A "Piece of Work"

In therapeutic jargon, one session or series of sessions in which a person deals with a particular anger is called a "piece of work." Once the excuses are eliminated, there is a process, a sequence of five basic steps, which must be completed in order to complete the anger.

Step One. Focus

Focusing on the anger is the first step. Much anger is blocked because we generalize it: "I hate the world" or "I can't stand this family" or "This job stinks," for example. In the first place, this is not true. Our anger involves specific people in the world, the city, at the job. Secondly, even if it were true, there is no way to take a chunk of anger that big and do anything with it.

We have to cut it down to "who" it is in the world, the family or the job that we hate or have anger toward. We must identify the person who is the focus of our blocked anger. It may be, and probably is, several people, but we must pick one — preferably the one toward whom we feel the most anger — in order to begin.

If we identify others, it is suggested we mentally tell them, "I'll get to you later." Only one anger can be processed at a time.

For many people, just identifying the source of anger brings a sense of release, even before they've done anything about it. We have seen countless numbers of people heave a sigh of relief after merely admitting, "I'm angry at my mother," for example.

This relief comes because they have finally begun work on the jigsaw puzzle of their lives; the open identification of a focused anger puts one of the pieces in place. The system also goes into a state of excitement because this first step opens up optimistic possibilities. If the system could talk at this point, it would probably say, "Phew, he/she finally owned up to something; now I can get in gear and help."

Step Two. Commitment

Commitment to do a piece of work is the next step. This means making a commitment to oneself that, "I'm ready to do something about this. I don't want to live this way a minute longer than I have to." Until a person moves from "I should" or "I want" to "I will," nothing is really going to happen.

Step Three. Action

This third step is when we put our money where our mouth is, so to speak; we move from talking to doing.

A person can talk and talk about a feeling but that doesn't provide any permanent relief. Only processing the feeling does that. We have to actively get into the emotion to heal the emotion.

Using Symbolism

In this action step, we can, if we choose, do the processing by experiencing and completing the emotion "symbolically."

There are many techniques for symbolic dealing, a number of which have been demonstrated throughout this course, such as the empty-chair encounter in which the person on whom our anger is focused is symbolically placed in the chair facing us.

The reason symbolism is so effective in dealing with emotions is that, through our symbolic actions, the system responds as if we were actually performing the action with the person in question.

As we have seen, the other person does not have to be within our presence to complete the anger. We can bring them to the anger session in any way we wish.

If the chair or similar technique is used, it is important to remember the principles discussed earlier such as using "I" language, standing with feet firmly planted on the floor and speaking out loud and with forceful intention.

Silent recitation of the anger statements doesn't work as well. It's also important to watch for a whine in the voice. Raising the voice — shouting — breaks the whining, complaining position and speeds up contact with hostile feelings. Swearing is often helpful in clearing the blockage. Any kind of safe, reasonable, symbolic physical act that can accompany the words also hastens the completion.

For athletes or persons who normally engage in any form of physical exercise, the athletic game or recreational exercise can be used as a mode for anger release. When playing tennis, for instance, we can place the image of a person's face on the ball and, everytime we hit it, repeat one of the anger or resentment statements directly to the face on the ball. This is not a new proposition. In the 1920s, noted psychiatrist Dr. Karl Menninger proposed the same thing.

An important distinction must be made here. There is a vast difference between just hitting a ball and trying to knock off its cover and, on the other hand, projecting an image of the resented person onto the ball first and using "I" language to express our feelings.

It is true that there is sometimes temporary relief through strenuous physical exercise. But wearing ourselves out with physical exertion merely gives us a false sense of relief. It is more likely fatigue that we are experiencing and, when the body rejuvenates, the anger is still there. This creates discouragement, which adds to the store of unpleasant feelings.

Another way of symbolically completing anger which works well for some people is to sit down and write a letter to the other party, using the "I" language and just writing until there is a sense of completion, then burning the letter and bidding the person goodbye as the anger goes up in smoke.

Dealing With the "Old" Person

We sometimes have unresolved anger at a person with whom, now, in the present, we have a very good relationship. Perhaps the person has had a dramatic change in his or her life since the time years ago when he or she hurt and angered us.

Perversely, though, the old anger crops up from time
to time — totally unrelated to what is going on in the
present. If this is the case, it is very important to deal
with the anger at the "old" person. It is ineffective to
try to release anger at that previous personality by
directing the anger at the new personality.

The way to solve this is to put the old person — who
used to do the hurtful things to us — in the empty chair
and to complete our anger with that person.

Then we can continue our relationship with the new
person unhampered by our old negative feelings.

For example, if we have anger at an alcoholic or
addictive parent, spouse or child who did very cruel
things when he/she was in the active stages of alcoholism or addiction but who now has been a sober,
loving parent, mate, son or daughter for many years,
we probably need to deal with unfinished anger at the
old person.

Put that old person in the empty chair. It is not being
disloyal. After you have done this, the "new" person
who is currently in your life will sense a difference in
your feelings and appreciate this.

One man, who was participating in group Anger
Therapy, was talking about his father when he suddenly stopped in mid-sentence. He said, "I feel like
gagging."

The group facilitator asked him to travel back in time
and sit in his highchair and then asked the man, "What
is happening?

The man said, "I remember 'shovels' of scrambled
eggs coming at me; my dad was pushing them at me."
The therapist said, "What would you like to do with
those eggs?"

He replied, "I'd like to cram them right down his
throat."

A dozen eggs were obtained and the group went
outside. They took along a large ottoman they used for

chair encounters, both as a seat on which to place the symbolic person and as a "chopping block" on which the anger could be beat out with a bataca while the anger was being verbally expressed.

They covered the ottoman with two large plastic trash bags and the man, who had large hands, took a handful of eggs and smashed them onto the plastic covering, grinding them down with his palm.

He was symbolically grinding those eggs into the face of his father — his "old" father, the father of his early childhood.

The eggs splattered in every direction, onto dirt and rock and weeds and flowers and, with the splattering, his anger scattered to the winds.

Any kind of symbolic act which allows the system to complete an act that didn't get completed when it originally happened provides relief for the system. It is similar to being hungry: When we are hungry, the stomach says, "Eat," and when we eat something, the stomach stops nagging at us. When we complete anger, we take care of the system's need for completion.

Step Four. Closure

Step four of the Anger Therapy process is closure. The system knows when it is time for closure; it experiences a sense of completion, of relief, of release.

It is not necessary when doing a piece of work to go through a play-by-play replay of every interaction we ever had with the person in question. It is only necessary to work until we get that first big sense of completion.

It is also not necessary, or possible, to complete everything at once. We must allow time for digestion and integration of the movements.

If we try to fit all the pieces of the puzzle into place at once, we may not get the full picture. What is important is to complete one specific piece of work, the piece we are currently working on. This is commonly accomplished in one to three exercise sessions. Then it is vital to allow time for "processing" of the results.

Most major pieces of work are done months and even years apart. When we have done a good chunk of work and have come to a natural stopping place, the system lets us know: "Things are in place; I feel great."

When one partner has completed anger alone, it is not necessary to recreate the anger again with the other party. A mere acknowledgment such as, "I dealt with my old anger about . . . and I wanted you to know that it's all taken care of" is all that is required for closure.

It is likely that, in two or three years, after we have grown and changed more, we will receive another message from our system that it is once again time to do a piece of major work.

The "message" is usually a feeling of not being as comfortable emotionally as we would like to be. Then, we identify the source of the current "nagging" and work on it until we once again have that sense of completion and accomplishment.

As each piece of work is completed, it is necessary to make closure. We do this by expressing, out loud, to the symbolic person what it is we have accomplished in the session. It makes us admit that we did make progress. After expressing that fact aloud, it will be difficult for us to deceive ourselves later and claim that we did not make progress.

Step Five. Self-Check and Integration

The fifth and final step in the Anger Therapy process begins with a self-check. We take a few minutes of quiet time to check ourselves out and ask ourselves: How am I feeling now physically? Emotionally? Intellectually? What am I feeling in all those areas since I did this piece of work? We then just let ourselves experience the feelings for a time. This starts the integration process, allowing the good feelings to be carried into everyday life.

These are the five steps that explain the dynamics of Anger Therapy. Now, let's look briefly at the therapy's origin and development.

Scientific Underpinnings of Anger Therapy

Anger Therapy has been adapted from experiential therapies such as the Gestalt Therapy of Fritz Perls, the psychodrama of J.L. Moreno, who was a colleague of Sigmund Freud's, and from role-playing techniques developed by Virginia Satir. It evolved to its present state through years of clinical application, in concert with academic refinement.

Anger Therapy is "specialty" therapy in which therapists receive advanced clinical training and coursework in the specialty of anger completion. The training is analogous to that which a medical doctor receives after graduation from medical school when he or she obtains specialty training in, for example, pediatrics, or surgery.

In Tucson, the Anger Therapy program is open to individuals who have completed a master's degree or a Ph.D. program in psychology or counseling and guidance or a related clinical field.

The training begins with an intensive University of Arizona workshop, offered at the graduate level, followed by two semesters of academic work and clinical training under the supervision of trained Anger Therapists.

One important course requirement is the involvement of students in intensive anger work of their own. It is vital that Anger Therapists first clear their own systems so they do not take their unfinished business into the therapy arena where it can get mixed in with the client's unfinished business.

As we learned at the beginning of the book, everyone has anger; therapists who have not completed their own major angers cannot provide significant assistance to others.

Anyone wishing further information on the program or desiring the name of a recommended Anger Therapist in a certain area of the country, may contact Dr. Roger J. Daldrup, c/o Living Business Press, P.O. Box 2007, Aptos, CA 95001-2007.

11

FREEDOM

Peace. Freedom. Enjoyment. Confidence. Vitality. These are among the rich rewards we start experiencing in our lives as we move from suppression and storage of anger to expression and release.

As we continue to keep the system clean and clear, we integrate these attributes into our being; they become part of us and we become more "whole."

To understand how this happens, let's consider the source of the new vitality and the other rewarding attributes. This source is energy.

One dictionary defines energy as "internal or inherent power" and "capacity of acting." Another definition says energy is "stored up power seeking to release itself."

When we complete our unfinished business, we regain, we re-own that inherent power.

Denying and repressing anger consumes our energy. Every time we go past a point in our lives without taking care of it, we have to leave a part of ourselves back there to tend it, to keep trying to complete it or cover it up.

Constantly leaving pieces of ourselves at those various way stations causes us to become more and more fragmented — and more drained. Tending to all those various pieces of ourselves that we parceled out along the way is a burdensome task.

Some of our energy is back there so it's not available to us here and now. Instead of energy, we experience apathy, inertia, boredom, lethargy. Usually, if we are in this state, we can't figure out why we are so worn out, so burned out.

Perhaps we consult a doctor who examines us and tells us there is nothing wrong. After the momentary relief passes, we still feel the same.

As more and more of these pieces of us are abandoned to the past, we also lose our sense of wholeness. Those pieces of ourselves scattered over our universe drain us of our sense of potency.

Self concept suffers, self esteem gets lower. We may not have the confidence to try new things.

We also may lose our sense of identity because we have lost so many pieces we don't know who we are. If we cut off pieces of ourselves for whatever reason, we lose ourselves, piece by piece.

Because we are "piecemeal persons" — out of balance persons — we may start relying on just one part of ourselves to get us through life. We may depend on our physical prowess, rely on our handsomeness or sex appeal, or upon our cognitive intellectual self.

Expecting one part of ourselves to do all the work puts us in a defensive position which means that we have to out-talk, outmaneuver others, play intellectual snob, be more clever, more socially adept, sexier, more everything to stay "even." Huge chunks of energy disappear.

As we bring ourselves back together into a whole, there are certain specific results which can be reliably predicted. Following is a list of some of these dynamics or "movements" of anger release that you can expect to experience if you have not already begun to do so.

Movement to Full-Range Response

This movement from a narrow, limited number of emotional responses to a full range allows us to experience the full scope of human emotions. We can experience joy and we can experience sadness; we can experience gentleness and we can experience confidence. We're not stuck at one end of the emotional scale.

When we move into this position of choosing from a variety of responses, we assume response-ability for our own life; we no longer pass off the responsibility to someone else.

Movement from Imbalance to Balance

This move to balance manifests in all our systems; it shows up in everything that is important in our lives. It can be seen in our handwriting, the way we drive a car, the way we encounter people physically, the way we meet and say hello to them, the way we walk across the room, the way we talk. It can be felt in our hugs.

Our emotional balance or imbalance also has a direct relation to the people and situations we draw into our life.

There is a natural attraction, a magnetism, between people who are operating on the same wave lengths. If ours is negative and counterproductive, we attract — and seek out — people who will reinforce our negative patterns.

This accounts, for instance, for the woman who marries one alcoholic husband after another or who goes from one unhealthy relationship to another, or for the child abuse victim who, in adult life, seeks situations which support continuance of the victim role.

Movement to Active Participation

Contact is the key word here. Once we stop lying to ourselves about how we feel — which is a tremendous relief — we make contact with other people. We don't run from the world, we run to it.

Instead of being the reactor, we now act upon.

Actually, now that we have both possibilities, we can choose to react or to be the actor. This is different from always being the reactor who has no seeming choice in the matter. This increases potency and, consequently, life begins to move more the way we want it to move.

Reclaiming Our Power

The new attitude becomes, "I'm capable, I can handle this and, even when I'm not handling something quite as I would like, I can survive it" (which is a way of handling).

All of the preceding movements have led to this development of potency, this expression of power in our life.

If we have processed and "dumped" all our old garbage, we can look at ourselves and say, "I'm not poisonous, I'm not toxic; I'm a nurturing and wholesome being."

Staying in Power

To remain in the nourishing state requires updating and maintenance.

Once we have done the major pieces of work on stored anger, we maintain emotional health by processing new angers in the here and now.

If we get in the habit of tending to our angers as they come up, they don't usually require much work; they haven't had time to settle in.

If our system is clear, we can say to someone, right when something is happening, "I don't like your saying that to me" or "I disagree with you." This will usually only be a split-second exchange in which nothing more is needed for completion than verbal acknowledgment of the feeling. Remember the dictum: The only valid reason for expressing anger is to get it out of the system.

If it is not socially or professionally appropriate to express at that moment, we can still deal with it in the now by making an appointment with ourselves to deal with it within the next few hours or days at a more appropriate time, such as after work or when the guests have gone.

The goal of Anger Therapy is to assist people in unblocking log jams in their emotional systems in a way that is healthy and productive rather than destructive. The objective is to clear the system, so it can be brought up to the present and to keep it updated by dealing with new angers before they get their hooks in us and become debilitating.

We all know that life isn't always going to go just as we would wish, but when we have the confidence, the wherewithal and the information, we can go through the dips and the downs and know we are going to come out OK on the other side.

We also have learned that the amount of time we spend in the dip is totally our choice. It is our right to have the dips and to stay in them as long as we wish and, when we are ready, to move from the down to the up position. We now have more tools with which to do this — tools that weren't before apparent and available to us.

When we have regained our energy, our inherent power, we can use that energy for whatever we wish: for enjoying sunsets, listening to music, appreciating our children, our relationships, study, exciting work, helping others, spiritual growth, travel, making love. The options are endless, and they are ours. This is freedom.

RELATED READINGS

1. Tim La Haye and Bob Phillips, **Anger Is a Choice,** Zondervan Publishing, Grand Rapids, Mich., 1982.

   The authors build a bridge between psychological and religious concepts of anger. Contains an "Irritability Quotient" from an anger inventory.

2. Elizabeth Weiss, **The Anger Trap,** Philosophical Library, 1984.

   Includes discussion of body language and also how anger affects the body: fatigue, headaches, stomach disorders, etc.

3. Linda Chierse, **The Wounded Woman,** Shanef-hala Press, London, 1983.

   This book about father-daughter relationships discusses the fallout when a daughter is rejected by her father at the time of puberty.

4. Daldrup, R. J., Beutler, L. E., Greenberg, L. S., & Engle, D. E., **Focused Expressive Psychotherapy: Helping Patients with Constricted Affect,** Guilford Publications, New York City, 1988.

   A detailed technical manual for therapists in training to learn the Anger Therapy treatment modality. Covers the theoretical principles underlying the practice role of counselor and client; dynamics of the model; process; techniques; and evaluation after treatment.

5. Robin Norwood, **Women Who Love Too Much,** Tarcher Inc., 1985.

   Helpful in assisting the reader to understand how people can become addicted to a dysfunctional relationship. Discusses methods for freeing self from such relationships.

6. Janet Geringer, **Adult Children of Alcoholics,** Woititz Health Communications Inc., Pampano Beach, Fla., 1983.
    Dealing with effects of growing up with alcoholic parent(s).

7. Fredericks Perls, **Gestalt Therapy Verbatim,** Real People Press, Lafayette, Ca., 1969.
    Illustrates the principles of Gestalt Therapy in a weekend demonstration group.

8. Eric Marcus, **Gestalt Therapy and Beyond,** Meta Publications, Cupertino, Ca., 1979.
    Principles of Gestalt Therapy are presented clearly in discussion and illustration. Understandable and theoretically sound.

9. Claudia Black, **Repeat After Me,** MAC printing and Publications, Denver, 1985.
    Good for investigating past causes of present discomfort. Best used in a pre-therapeutic setting so material which is uncovered can be dealt with more effectively in therapy.

10. **Marty Mann's New Primer on Alcoholism,** Henry Holt & Co., New York, an Owl Book (updated version, 1981).

11. Edited by S.L. Garfield and A.E. Bergin, **Handbook of Psychotherapy and Behavioral Change,** Wiley Publisher, New York City, 1986.
    More than 1,000 studies summarized on the relationship of process to outcome in psychotherapy. See especially chapters by David E. Orlinsky and Kenneth I. Howard who discuss the important variables in the successful outcome of psychotherapy. These variables include having the patient "do" something rather than just talk about the problem, and the beneficial effects of focusing on feelings.

For information on general-interest or special-focus anger management seminars and workshops in your area, write to:

> Dodie Gust Anger Management Center
> 2701 California Avenue
> Suite 217
> Seattle, Wash. 98116

> or:

> Dr. Roger J. Daldrup
> c/o Living Business Press
> P.O. Box 2007
> Aptos, CA 95001-2007

For information on the batacas (see page 60), call or write:

> Living Business Press
> P.O. Box 2007
> Aptos, CA 95001-2007
> (408) 722-6240

St. Louis Community College
at Meramec
Library